TARBUCK
ON GOLF

TARBUCK
ON GOLF

Illustrations by Richard Willson
Foreword by Tony Jacklin

RETRO CLASSICS

**This book is dedicated to Henry Cotton, whose friendship and
company I have enjoyed so very much, and whose ears
I have bruised in my search for golfing knowledge.**

RETRO CLASSICS
is a collection of facsimile reproductions
of popular bestsellers from the 1980s and 1990s

Tarbuck on Golf was first published in 1983 by Willow Books

Re-issued in 2012 as a Retro Classic
by G2 Entertainment
in association with Lennard Publishing
Windmill Cottage
Mackerye End
Harpenden
Hertfordshire
AL5 5DR

Copyright © Jimmy Tarbuck 1983

ISBN 978-1-909040-31-1

Produced by Lennard Books
a division of
Lennard Associates Limited

Editor Michael Leitch
Designed by David Pocknell's Company Ltd

Printed and bound by Lightning Source

CONTENTS

FOREWORD

Jimmy Tarbuck and I have been friends for a very long time now – and I mean really good friends. I do not think we have had a cross word in the fifteen or so years we have known each other. One of the reasons for that is, I suppose, the mutual respect we have for each other's achievements.

Through golf Jimmy has found a whole new audience for his talents, which means of course that far more people are able to enjoy his great humour. What a lot of people probably don't appreciate is how hard he has had to work at his golf game over the years to achieve his 4 handicap, which must be the lowest in showbiz.

I know you are going to enjoy the feast of stories he has to tell in this book. I see I am involved in a few of them myself. After your laughter has subsided, please remember it was all made possible through this great game of golf.

JIMMY TARBUCK ... THIS IS YOUR GOLF

At the end of the last show in the first series of *Live From Her Majesty's,* I was ambushed by Eamonn Andrews carrying his Big Red Book. The next two hours were total confusion. I know that because I looked up 'confusion' in the dictionary: it said 'Father's Day in Harlem'. All credit, though, to Eamonn and his researchers, who had undoubtedly got my priorities right. Together with all the family and friends, three Open champions appeared on the programme: Tony Jacklin, Gary Player and Henry Cotton.

I was very flattered that they had come along. What is more, the stories they told made a neat summary of so much that I find attractive about the game of golf – the fun, the competition, the sunshine and beautiful surroundings.

First, the fun. Tony Jacklin remembered an incident during the Lancôme tournament in Paris. We were staying in the same hotel, and one morning I thought I would ring him in his room.

'Hello,' he answered.

'Ello. M'sieu Jackleen?' I inquired in my best Parisian's English. 'Zis ees ze Paris Match magazine. We would like ver' merch to 'ave some photographs taken wiz you . . .'

'Yes', said Tony. 'That's not a problem.'

I went on: 'Do you like to be photographed . . . ?'

'Not when I'm playing,' said Tony firmly.

'Non, non,' I cried. 'We understand zat. But we must arrange ze rendezvous. Tell me, do you practeese *before* you play?'

'Yes,' replied Tony. 'Yes, that would be a good time.'

'Good,' I said. 'Tell me, do you practeese *after* you play?'

'No,' said Tony.

The voice of Tarbuck came down the phone. 'Well you should. You'd win more bloody tournaments!'

'Yaaarrgh!' cried the voice of Jacklin at the other end of the line. 'I'll get you . . .'

Next, the competition. Gary Player also recalled the Lancôme event, in which he and his French partner were drawn against myself and Tony Jacklin. Unfortunately, Gary remembered, his French and his partner's English were not at all compatible; in fact all he ever got from his partner was 'Oui, oui.'

We played our match, with a side-stake of £50. I played well, Jacklin played well, and my team beat Player's team 6 and 5. Despite Gary's efforts the Frenchman could do very little to help.

'Never mind "oui oui",' said Gary. 'We were *peed on* from a great height!'

Finally, the sunshine and the beautiful surroundings, represented on the show by Henry Cotton, squire of Penina in the Algarve, where I have spent many happy hours playing and, afterwards, chatting with the great man.

Penina, with Vale do Lobo, is one of the first two courses in the Algarve that Henry himself designed, and it has all the warmth and elegance that I associate with the very best in 'Sunshine Golf'. Some years ago I went there with Ronnie Corbett, and on

one particular morning Henry was booked up with lessons and could not come round with us. However, to make sure we weren't neglected, Henry led out a much-loved donkey, called Pacifico, and introduced him to us.

'You don't need to worry,' Henry assured us. 'Pacifico will accompany you, carry your clubs, show you the way. Just let Pacifico look after you.'

On the first tee Ronnie Corbett could no longer hide his emotions. 'Wasn't that *sweet* of Henry to give us this lovely Pacifico?' he exclaimed, patting the donkey, a serene and grateful smile spreading all over his face. I thought he was going to cry.

It was Pacifico himself who restored the balance. First, with no warning at all, he watered the tee fiercely, standing stock-still until he had unloaded about ten gallons on the playing area. Then, apparently feeling he had contributed enough, he ambled off, first walking, then trotting – with our clubs strapped to his back!

'Oi! Come back!' we shouted. 'Oi! You with the big ears! Come back *this minute!*'

Clip–clop, clip–clop. The donkey took not a blind bit of notice. He nipped round the side of a grassy bank and disappeared.

'You bloody Pacifico!' we were soon shouting. 'Come back. Oi! Come back!'

My abiding memory of that day is of little Ronnie Corbett sprinting towards the horizon in pursuit of this evil donkey who had just nicked his clubs. As always, of course, Corbett took it in good heart, and later made a donation to the home for retired donkeys at Hatfield: Pacifico.

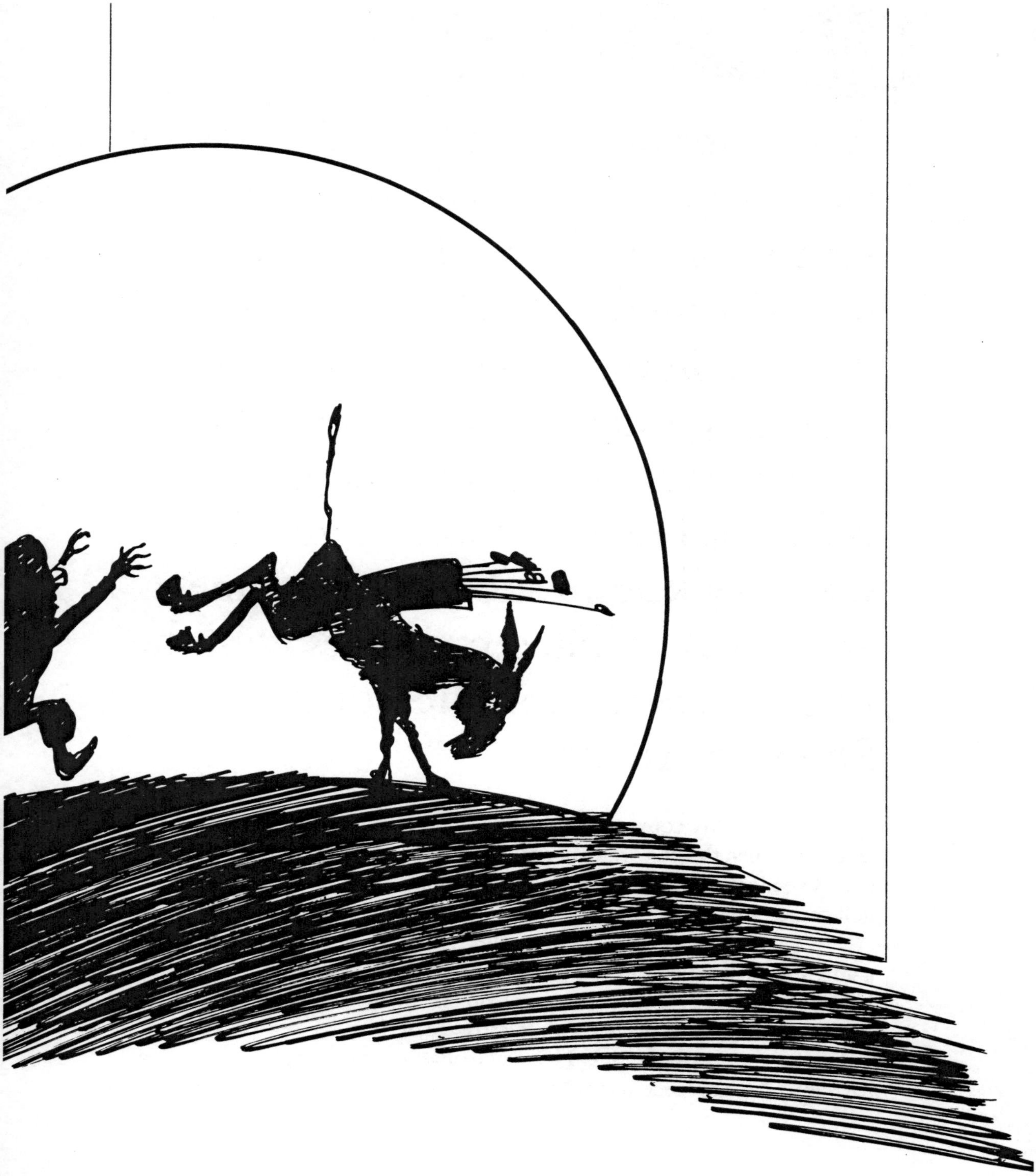

WHY GOLF?

It might well have been football. In fact, I am surprised it turned out to be anything else, especially after my Liverpool childhood. In Liverpool the majority view – at school, at work, in the pub, in the street – is that anyone more interested in a sport other than football is either insane or a pervert. Not that I resisted football; in fact I was very keen. I still love the game, and have exhibited my knees with the finest in charity matches for the Showbiz All Stars.

My conversion to golf was a gradual process. People have asked me when the bug really bit, but I am not convinced it works quite like that. The more I think about it, the only toothmarks I have ever seen on a golf course are the ones on the neck of Christopher Lee's caddie.

Bugs may bite some golfers, but to me the qualities of the game, and its pleasures, are not things that you suddenly latch onto in some blinding moment of truth. They creep up on you more slowly, and you appreciate them more deeply with the passage of time.

Looking back, I can say that golf – even more than showbiz – has allowed me to meet, *and* get to know, *and* compete against, people of every social rank and belief. I have played the game with royalty, with presidents, with publicans, taxi-drivers, ministers, MPs, footballers – and with countless great golf professionals. Golf has influenced my life to such an extent that I honestly do not know what I would have done otherwise with my time. My profession is littered with casualties who never found something to occupy them during all those free afternoons that are an inescapable part of our life – especially on tour when the gentle landlady shoos everyone out in the morning and keeps the front door bolted until 5 pm.

However, if anyone had predicted even half of my involvement with golf on the day, long ago, when I went to Allerton Municipal course for my first ever game, I would have told them to take their magic lamp, fill it with cement and drop it in the Mersey . . . or words to that effect.

In those days a round at the Municipal cost two and sixpence, including the hire of the clubs. You paid another two bob for three balls – usually shapeless, cut-up things – and round you went, hacking and bashing the ball until it was too tired and bruised to argue further, and dropped into the hole. My first opponent was a friend called Roger Heath, and then I met the Large family who are very well known in golf circles. Bill Large was the assistant pro at the Allerton course.

Although Bill is himself a fine player, you will get a better idea of the average playing standard from a story which Bill told me. Nearly all his customers hired their clubs, and these were kept in separate bags in the shop. For some reason they had one bag which was always used for storing 7-irons; nothing but 7-irons. One day Bill was out and the young junior was alone in the shop when a player came in to hire a bag of clubs. The junior, not knowing any better, handed him the bag containing fourteen 7-irons.

When Bill came back he noticed the 7-iron bag was missing. The junior innocently explained that he had just hired the bag out. 'Christ!' thought Bill, 'that man will be raving potty by now.' He settled down rather uneasily to wait, and eventually the punter was sighted approaching the 18th green with a face as black as thunder. He clattered into the pro's shop.

'How can anyone play with these clubs?' he yelled.

'Yes, yes,' said Bill. 'I quite agree . . .'

'You gave me all these clubs,' continued the angry punter, gesturing at the bag. 'But you forgot the bloody putter!'

The poor soul had driven and chipped his way all round the 15 course with 7-irons, but then had felt cheated because he had no putter!

A great friend of mine later in the Fifties was Bobby Campbell, now manager of Portsmouth FC. Bobby, who was to be best man at my wedding, is a great natural athlete and in those summers at Allerton, when he was playing for Liverpool, he used to go round maybe three times a day, whittling his handicap down to about five.

The 18th on the top course at Allerton is a short four. In those days it seemed to us a mighty four, but Campbell was not easily daunted.

16

Beside the fairway was a hut where players changed their shoes before going out to play. My favourite incident from that course is seeing Campbell hit a huge slice with his driver. In vain he bellowed 'Fore!' as the ball arrowed straight for the open door of the hut and screamed inside. From where we stood, we could hear the ball ricocheting off the wooden walls of the hut – bing! boing! bing! Suddenly, three fellers came hurtling out the door, like terrified soldiers deserting a machine-gun nest which someone had just stuffed with hand grenades.

'Bloody Campbell!' they shouted, as we tried not to laugh.

17

The Gorleston murders

For some years after I went into show business, golf remained low in my priorities. As a sport I still preferred football, and my golf anyway wasn't so much golf as hacking a small ball round a bumpy field, scuffing it along for nine or ten shots per hole. Then in 1964 I joined Dickie Henderson in a show at the Coventry Hippodrome. He said: 'Do you play golf?' I said: 'I have done.' The upshot was, I bought a pair of golf shoes and started going round with him. Dickie, who does a great deal of charity work and likes to take his time over everything, exhibited saintly patience and got me really keen on the game.

This set me up well for the following year, when I went into a summer show at Great Yarmouth. Amongst our crowd the natural meeting place seemed to be Gorleston Golf Club, where George Willard was the pro. I bought my first set of clubs from George, and he suggested that I play a round or two with his daughter, Anne.

Anne was only fourteen at the time, but she had just won the British Girls' championship. She took me out and played me for golf balls. She gave me a stroke a hole – and murdered me. Then she gave me a stroke a hole, and two strokes on the par fives. The result was the same: murder. This was all a bit hard on J Tarbuck, then the up-and-coming comic, and I used to go quietly, and sometimes noisily, bananas while this little girl destroyed me. At the time I just could not *understand* how it was possible for her to do what I so obviously could not. Anne is now married and we laugh about it when we meet, but at the time there was no-one in the world who could make me more infuriated.

Later in 1965 I got the job of compering at the Palladium, and through that winter and the following spring I had to concentrate on my stage work. Golf took a back seat until the summer, when I received an invitation to play in a big pro-am at Sunningdale.

I was delighted. I was drawn with Harry Weetman and a feller called Anthony Tate. At the 1st tee they drove off beautifully and I, who had never played golf in front of such a multitude, almost killed someone standing at the end of the tee.

While I struggled to control my nerves and put some sort of game together, Mr Tate proved to be a charming companion. He said:

'I hear you come from Liverpool.'

'Yes,' I said.

'What part of Liverpool?'

'Well,' I replied, 'I was brought up in Wavertree, and I have a great friend, Bobby Campbell, who used to live down Scotland Road.'

'Oh,' he said. 'Scotland Road. We have a business there.'

It seemed an unlikely place – down by the docks in Liverpool – for such a well-mannered gentleman to have some kind of business connection.

'Really?' I said. ' *You* do?'

'Yes,' he said, 'it's a family business.'

'Oh,' I said, 'what's it called?'

'Tate and Lyle.'

At the time my brother was working for them driving a wagon. 'Bloody hell,' I said. 'I'm playing with Royalty!'

First pots

That was my initiation into pro-ams, and since then I have played in pro-am competitions all over the world. Gradually, the attractions of golf in all its forms were getting a hold on me. Bobby Campbell, Dickie Henderson, Anne Willard, the Sunningdale pro-am . . . the conspirators were many and various. For a while the demands of the Palladium show took up most of my time, then in summer 1967 I went up to Blackpool for the season and for the first eight weeks, before the kids broke up from school and our families arrived, I shared a house with Bruce Forsyth. We played golf every day, and that was the time when, at last, my game began to improve.

The highlight of the whole summer was winning my first pro-am, at Royal Lytham and St Anne's. I was partnered by the great Christy O'Connor, and he came on stage that night at the theatre. I had been 19 unable to attend the party at the golf club because I had to be back in Blackpool for the first house. In the interval Christy appeared down the aisle, climbed up on the stage and presented me with my trophy. A lovely moment.

Having reached this high point in the story of my golfing life, I can now reveal with greater dignity that this was not the first trophy I had won. The very first trophy I ever won was the Show Business Rabbits Cup, and I captured it at Gorleston in 1965. In a tense final I was matched against Norman Vaughan. We lived up to the name of the trophy in every aspect of our game. Norman knocked his ball round in 125, and I beat him, thrillingly, by one shot.

I became a member of Coombe Hill Golf Club, and there came within the sphere of influence of Dick Burton, a marvellous professional. Under his caustic gaze my handicap of 18 was ground down over the next two years until it reached single figures.

Dick was a larger-than-life character who liked to win. One day he partnered the club captain in a Guildford alliance meeting. They played well, especially Dick, and when they came to the 18th tee they needed a four to win Dick a prize of £100. He hit a superb drive and turned cheerfully to his partner:

'Just get me on the green, Mr Captain,' he said. 'We've got this one. Hundred pound. Very handy.'

The club captain obliged him by topping the second shot into a bunker. Steam was coming out of Dick Burton's ears as he strode towards the ball. He snatched up a 4-iron, closed the face, and smashed the ball deep into the sand wall at the front of the bunker, burying it by about an arm's length. He swung round on his partner.

'Right, Mister Captain,' he snarled. 'Get that out!'

The captain, later in the day, commented: 'I'll *never* play with that man again!'

U and non-U

You can't go far in golf without coming up against the laws of etiquette. These, as distinct from the rules of the game, are more concerned with the way you conduct yourself on the course.

For the most part the laws of etiquette are based on common sense and the fact that life rolls on more smoothly if people try to be pleasant and polite to each other. On the other hand, life would be very boring if there were

20

never any outbursts like that of Dick Burton in the bunker. Take away the passion, and who would want to play? Not, certainly, the people I would choose as partners and opponents.

With an attitude such as mine, it is inevitable that occasional light skirmishes have to be fought on the etiquette front. Not long ago, I was going round with a friend at Coombe Hill and we came up behind two ladies of a certain age. We watched with superb patience as they tacked along one of the short holes, eventually zig-zagging to the green in five. Realizing that we would be lucky to finish before nightfall if we stayed behind them, I called out politely:

'Ladies! Ladies! May we come through?'

One of the ladies turned round and in very stern tones said: 'You'll wait. You'll wait, because this is a *Ladies'* competition.'

Alas, this was too much for me. I could not help calling back: 'Well, dear, the way you're playing, you've got *no* chance of winning.'

When we came in, I was hauled up in front of the secretary. Knuckles were rapped.

'Does the truth hurt?' I asked, in mild protest.

The secretary made choking noises and said: 'Yes. Er. Hum.

But you mustn't say that to the ladies.'

The lady herself returned to the locker-room, still fuming from the incident. Pauline, my wife, happened to be in there as well, standing on the other side of the lockers.

'That Jimmy Tarbuck is a *very* rude man,' complained the lady to her companion.

Pauline called out: 'You're quite right. And I've lived with him for twenty years!'

Drinks all round

My wife is now a very respectable player, with a handicap of 13. At first I think she took up the game because it seemed better to join it than fight it; but she has done extremely well. A few months back, she had a hole in one. I got to the clubhouse afterwards and everyone said:

'Congratulations.'

I said: 'Why?'

'Your wife has had a hole in one.'

I said: 'That's marvellous. I'm delighted.'

The barman said: 'May I present you with this bar bill?'

'No you may not,' I replied. 'See her. Nothing to do with me.' The nerve of the man. I mean, etiquette and all that. Got to do things properly.

22

23

THE SAYINGS OF DENIS

First, a word of introduction to these sayings which you will find sprinkled through the book; and to Denis himself. Denis is a good steady club player. He is also a hopeless optimist, and I am not sure whether that makes him more typical of the average club golfer, or less. But to me his great and enduring strength is that, on the golf course, he is totally committed to the world of If Only and What Might Have Been. I'll give you an example:

Denis: 'I hit that *beautifully.*'

A Friend: 'Where are you, Denis?'

Denis: 'In the lake.'

A Friend: 'In the lake?'

Denis: 'Yes. But I hit it *right* in the middle of the club.'

SPORTING CHANCES

The official stepped briskly forward at the first tee. Behind him a black-clad figure, known to millions of golf

watchers throughout the world, also walked forward, but a little more casually; both hands, one gloved, hung loose. The official raised his clipboard, and in his Sunday-best voice, which sounded as if he was compering *Songs of Praise* from The Mansion House, declaimed:

'Gary Player. US Masters. US Open. US PGA. British Open. South African Open. Brazilian Open. Australian Open. Dunlop Masters. Waikiki Open. Piccadilly World Match Play. Canada Cup. This Open. That Open . . .'

A couple of people in the gathering at the first tee cast looks of surprised disdain over the man drawn to play with this great professional. Me. Catching their lofted eyebrows, I mumbled defensively: 'Well, he *is* meant to be very good, you know.' The lofted eyebrows swung away. No-one said: 'Quite,' but I could hear it in the air.

Gary Player addressed his opening ball. Bonk! It soared up in a perfect arc, parallel with the open beach to the right, then curved slightly left with the prevailing wind to land plumb in the centre of the fairway. The generous applause from those around the tee was followed by half a minute's silence while the official ran a finger down his clipboard. When at last he had found his place he announced, in clipped Ayrshire tones:

'Jimmy Tarbuck. Coombe Hill.'

I stepped forward. Smash! The ball

rocketed out knee-high and veering left, dangerously close to the thick rough guarding that side of the fairway. Still, never mind, I thought. I hadn't played an airshot. I hadn't hit anybody. Most important of all we were, at last, away and started on the first round of golf I had ever played with a great international star.

That is one of the marvels of golf. Thanks to the handicapping system, it is the only game where an ordinary amateur player can walk the course and compete with the greatest exponents in the world. However much we may admire tennis players such as Jimmy Connors or Bjorn Borg, we will never have a chance of playing them at Wimbledon. The same is true of football – imagine trying to dummy past Hoddle or Dalglish at Wembley. In fact, I can't think of any other game where you can play the pros on an equal footing.

It will cost you a bit, of course. But golf is a super-sport, and the pros have to be financed somehow, otherwise they would not come. At the same time, there are great benefits to be earned on behalf of the many deserving charities which receive large donations from pro-am tournaments.

From my own experience, I believe I am still the only person in showbiz to have a special clause written into his contract stipulating that the Aforementioned must have one Saturday off in the middle of a summer season. That was in 1970, the year I met Gary Player. I was doing a summer season in Bournemouth, Sean Connery was organizing a two-day tournament at Troon, and it was Sean who telephoned with the news that I had been drawn with Gary Player. I hired a plane, flew up at dawn to Scotland, missed the Saturday night show – they had to put in a deputy – played the match and flew back to Bournemouth on the Monday.

Never mind the panic

Was it worth it? Of course it was worth it. Nerves and all. If you suffer from Golf Fever, you would never stop kicking yourself if you turned down an opportunity like that.

It is a feeling which reverberates all round the pro-am circuit. I recently had a frantic phone call from a good friend – a 24-handicap player – who was in the Bob Hope Classic.

'I've just had the draw,' he wailed at me. 'I'm drawn against Telly Savalas and Brian Barnes – on the first day!'

'Great,' I said. 'That should be really good.'

'No,' he cried. 'How am I going to handle it? I mean, what do you think I should do?'

The note of panic was unmistakeable – and familiar. I thought of my own daunting initiation, of the huge crowds that follow the Bob Hope event, the vast galleries around the greens.

'There's only one thing for it,' I said. 'Just play your natural game – and take a pair of brown corduroy trousers!'

I also remember when Lou Freedman was feeling his way in the pro-ams. One day he was drawn with Tony Jacklin and Neil Coles. A large crowd turned up and Lou felt very nervous when he went out to the 1st tee. Jacklin picked some grass and threw it in the air.

'Give me a 4-iron,' he said to his caddie.

Neil Coles tossed his grass in the air.

'I'll hit a 3-iron,' he said to his caddie.

Lou Freedman threw his grass in the air.

'Caddie,' he said, 'go and buy me another cashmere sweater.'

New dreamers: start here

No school speech day is complete without some pinstriped mobster reminding the lads that it is enough to have taken part sportingly, to have battled valiantly, etc. This message is particularly welcome if the school 1st team are a load of deadbeats who haven't won a match all season. But when you get amongst the fringes of professional sport, you see a different world. Here the aim is to beat the rest. For the amateur golfer, the best thing about this is: with a bit of luck, he can actually play with the best *and* have his own brief snatches of glory. If he does, he will never forget them for the rest of his life.

Not surprisingly, I should like to tell you about one of my own peaks. It happened at the Bob Hope Classic. On the last day, on a par-four, I holed a five-iron shot for a two. Streaky it may have been, but a great roar went up, and even though I was playing the nine holes that were not being covered by the television cameras, word got through and they announced that 'Jimmy Tarbuck's had a two net one on a par four.' It gave me a tremendous thrill, and provoked Howard Clark, the professional going round with me, to point wonderingly at my miracle-working five-iron and say: 'Can I buy that?'

At such moments you quit the ranks of the bumbling hopefuls, and become one of the *real* golfers. Heady stuff. Nearly as good as playing with Arnold Palmer, as I once did in a pro-am event in the United States, and in the locker-room afterwards was told by the great man, then and now a close relative of the Almighty in American sporting circles: 'I enjoyed that. Shall we go and have a drink?'

Invisible jets of air lifted my feet a clear six inches off the locker-room floor, and I hovercrafted all the way to the bar at the shoulder of Arnold Palmer. ARNOLD PALMER!?!!

Ranking almost with my superb five-iron shot is a 33-yard putt knocked in by Terry Wogan while he was playing in the Pro-Celebrity golf series. Quite rightly, he still hasn't stopped broadcasting and writing

about it. But to my mind it isn't always the wonder shot that pulls most at the viewer's heart-strings. Anyone who saw Ronnie Corbett's Great Miss will surely agree. Again the Hope Classic was the venue. Ronnie, a nifty 16-handicapper, struck a beautiful tee shot which went on and on, and stopped at the most agonizing place you could possibly conceive – about a turn of the ball away from the hole. Had that ball gone in, the charity would have benefitted by some £20,000.

Fortunately Ronnie had fallen in a divot at the time and was prevented from seeing his ball stop short. When they pulled him out, it was all over. I think in a way that helped to soften the blow of having not quite hit a shot which he could have videoed and played back to himself for the rest of his days.

Apples of my eye

It is a marvel to me how the best of the pros manage to preserve a sense of the ridiculous, even at the most difficult moments. One of the characteristics of a great sportsman must be that he never lets himself be so overwhelmed by the gravity of the situation, or the enormity of the stakes he is playing for, that he fails to forget one essential truth: he is playing a game – and a pretty bloody daft one at that.

Let me give you an example of what we might call the humour of the absurd, and how it works. I was playing in a Texaco pro-am at Southport and Ainsdale. Well, not so much playing as making up the numbers because it was my lot to be going round with Tony Jacklin, just a year after he had won the US and British Opens, and Dr David Marsh, one of the only Englishmen to captain a winning Walker Cup side. What is more, David was playing at his home club, where he was enormously popular.

Consequently, we had a huge gallery following us round. We arrived on one of the greens, when Tony Jacklin suddenly shook me from the daze I had been living in since the first hole.

'Hey, JT,' he called. 'What's the line on this putt?'

Eh, whassat? I shook myself awake. What's he asking me for? Out loud I said: 'Why don't you ask David? After all, it's his home course. He can tell you far better than I can.'

'No,' said Tony. 'I want you to tell me.'

I walked across the green, a large one, and with several hundred pairs of eyes following me got down on one knee and began to examine the line of Tony's putt. Then Tony came over. He too got down on one knee, and said to me, in a kind of confidential murmur:

'Look at the knockers on that bird in the red over there.'

I looked. He was right. The ball was forgotten as our eyes fixed themselves on this utterly voluptuous woman dominating that side of the green. As we stared, I suddenly started laughing. I couldn't help it. Here I was, kneeling on a piece of Lancashire turf with God's gift to British and European golf, who was then competing seriously in a £10,000 tournament, and all he wanted to tell me about was this pair of . . .

What it must have looked like to the other spectators, I will never know. Except, that is, for the snarling boyfriend of the wonderful lady. From where he stood, just behind her, there could have been little doubt about what was holding up play.

Great heavens . . . they were big, though.

IN GOLF THE TRUTH

Golf is a double-edged game. It has the power to fascinate both as a sport of marvellous variety and as a daunting test of character. At a time when sportsmanship in other games is slipping – in football, for instance, in tennis, cricket and Rugby Union – golf has retained its high ideals as a true game of life, demanding total honesty.

34

You get the rulebenders, of course, and the fantasy merchants who lie about their handicaps – and I have a few stories to tell about them later in this chapter. But what to me makes golf outstanding is that, played as it should be played, it compels people to disclose their innermost selves in a way that I believe is unique in sport. If you take the old Latin saying 'In vino veritas', substitute golf for wine and translate it into English, you have a new saying that is no less meaningful: 'In golf the truth'.

Eighteen holes of golf, a few glasses of wine – each has the same compelling effect. The mask slips; the person is revealed.

I find it endlessly compelling to observe other golfers and how they react to triumphs and difficulties – difficulties mostly. Look at that businessman in the rough. Is he the sort you wouldn't trust on his own in a wood? The sort who is always stubbing his toe on the ball by accident, and moving it to a better lie? Just think: if he abuses the rules on the golf course, what would he be like to deal with in business?

'I know ze rules!'

My own interpretation of the rules fell like so much water off the back of an old Swedish duck I once met on the Costa del Sol. I had been drawn against her in a Stableford for the Casino Cup. This poor old soul had as much chance of winning as the donkey in the next field, but she was happy in her way.

As I stood and watched, she went into a bunker and with her club started patting down the sand behind her ball. Not once, but ten or a dozen times she patted the sand until it was nicely compacted. Always the gentleman, I tried at first to pretend I was looking the other way and hadn't seen her. But in the end, because she was being so downright obvious, I thought it would be stupid of me if I didn't say something.

I waited until she had set up a nice firm lie, and duly flopped the ball out of the bunker, and then I went up to her and said:

'Excuse me, madam, I think I should point out that you are not allowed to ground your sand wedge.'

'I know ze rules!' she cried. 'Zat's vy I take 9-iron . . .'

The invisible handicap

A more deliberate form of self-delusion is to play off a falsely high handicap. Some players who do this are out-and-out pothunters; they never enter a medal round, where they would be shown up, and the net result is that they succeed only by fiddling a system that was devised to give more people a better opportunity. To me that is not just selfish, it is completely crazy.

Every golf club also has its share of gloryseekers, or would-be Single Figure Men. Their trick is to say that they have a handicap of eight, when in fact they couldn't keep to fourteen. There is only one thing in favour of this group: they are wonderful opponents in matchplay events, where their pride makes them certain losers. All through the game, and afterwards in the bar, they splutter and complain:

'Not on my game today. Can't hit *anything* right.'

It is a kindness not to point out to them that they haven't been on their game for twenty years!

Under the influence

Unnecessary problems also arise when people take themselves too seriously. I am all for challenge and commitment, but one of my chief dislikes in the game today is that fairly new phenomenon, the five-and-a-half-hour round. I loathe playing them. I cannot concentrate that long, and I don't wish to. I get bored, and I don't mind saying so.

The problem must have its roots in professional golf, where rounds have been getting progressively longer. Now the habit has passed to amateurs, partly through the pro-am events, still more through watching golf on television. The trouble is, you need only a few slowcoaches out on the course at any one time to snarl up the whole works. With the pros it is possible to understand, even if you do not condone, their studied 'method school' of playing; they have a great deal at stake, ultimately their careers and livelihoods. But if amateurs start thinking this is the way to play, something is wrong. Not only are they taking themselves far too seriously, they are fiddling indecently with the future of the game at club level. I am all for commitment, as I said earlier, but it has to be fun too. Take away the fun, and it ceases to be golf as I want to know it.

I have a friend who is very keen on worm casts. Under winter rules he knows they can be a bonus to him, in fact it sometimes seems as if his entire game is built round his booming second shots taken from the tops of these handy little cones of mud. It's become a standing joke now.

'You can place it if you want to,' we shout to him.

36

'Yes, I know,' he says, selecting his driver. 'I already have.' Boom. The ball rockets away from the mound. Thank you very much. (Driver off a fairway in February? I ask you!)

It's best not to be too serious at such times. You have to draw the line somewhere, of course, between enthusiastic overinterpretation of the rules and downright misinterpretation. Take the man who lands on a slightly soggy patch of ground, then jumps four feet in the air all over it and claims casual water. You should only be able to claim casual water when the stuff is seeping up round your feet as you stand there, not after you have privately reorganized the landscape!

No rabbit like an old rabbit
In another episode, this time involving a player so well known I shall avoid naming him, I was an official scorer in one of the Piccadilly tournaments, before it became the Suntory. I was out with this eminent professional, and his equally eminent partner, when to my astonishment he walked up to his ball, looked down at it, turned to the referee and claimed:

'Rabbit scrape.'

In other words, he wanted to persuade the official that a rabbit had made an impression in the ground that gave him an unfair lie. The referee was John Thornhill, a very experienced official and former international player. He bent down, gave the ball a brief examination, and said:

'Rabbit scrape, eh? All right. We'll grant that.' Then he added, straightening up and turning to the eminent pro, 'But I should also like you to know that it was made by a *very old* rabbit.'

Henry Longhurst had the best answer. One of his favourite remarks was that the rules of golf should be so simple they could be written on a box of matches. Meanwhile, until someone got round to drafting this miraculous work, he offered this advice:

'You hit the ball, you hit it again, and you don't pick it up until you are on the green.'

I'll settle for that.

CHOOSE YOUR WEAPONS

In the matter of golfing equipment, I believe that the things we noticed at school hold true in later life. Then – it happened time after time – you could guarantee that the kid with the whitest shirt, the whitest trousers, the whitest boots and pads, could not play cricket to save his life. Nothing made me happier, if I was on the fielding side, than to see one of those Persil-sniffers coming out to bat. You could guarantee he would not last long; he never did.

It was the same with football. The boy with the shiny immaculate boots was certain to have shins like burglar alarms: one tap and he was off. Nowadays, on the golf course, especially at the pro-ams, the place is seething with equally useless individuals, got up like tailor's dummies. They wear Cashmere sweaters, Jacobson slacks, Footjoy shoes, leather gloves sensuous enough to wear to a bondage convention . . . As for their golf bags, we can only be thankful that the R & A decided, in 1939, to limit a full set of clubs to fourteen; otherwise, like Lawson Little of beloved

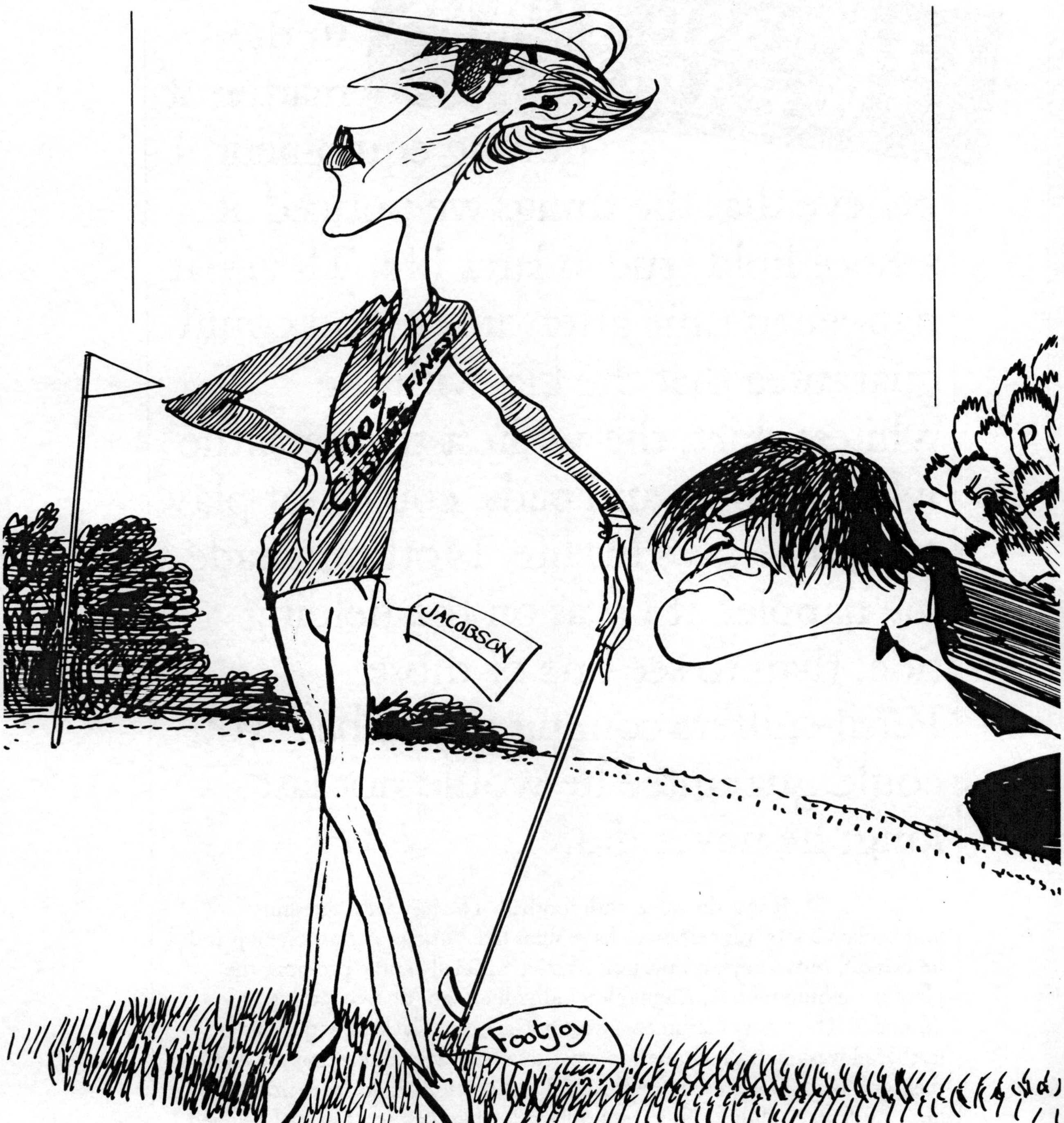
100% CASHMERE FINEST
JACOBSON
Footjoy

memory, they would want to take at least twenty-three round with them. As it is, their bags are twice as big as yours and mine, bulging with enough tackle for a fortnight's fishing holiday.

I am not averse, mind you, to the odd piece of neat equipment myself. To go further, I regard pro shops as Aladdin's caves, and am very unlikely to come out of one without having bought something. Dickie Henderson has the same problem. One day, knowing he had been drawn with Tony Jacklin in a pro-am tournament, he went out and bought some really immaculate gear: crocodile shoes, a camel hair sweater, goatskin slacks . . . Looking at himself in the full-length mirror at the shop, he thought he had never seen such a delightful outfit.

Came the day, and off he went to the golf club. In the locker-room he ran into Tony Jacklin. Jacklin was looking immaculate. He wore goatskin shoes, a crocodile sweater, camel hair slacks . . .

With clubs I am more serious, more of traditionalist. I believe that a golfer is what he is, and that once he has found clubs that suit his game, he should stick to them. Consequently, I do not shuttle about from one make or type to another. I tried the graphite shafts, but they did not work for me: I could hit the ball farther, but less consistently in the direction I wanted it to go. In general, I am impervious to heavy selling spiels, and to ads that shout about 'heel and toe, wonder flange, twisted insert to give you more height . . . hit low and you'll never shank again', etc, etc. What really happens, in my experience, is that when you are under pressure the ball may go anywhere – and nothing will have less influence on your shot than the make of club you use, no matter how many

magical properties it is cracked up to possess.

There are three important clubs in the bag: the driver, the wedge and the putter. You can fiddle with the rest – if you must fiddle at all. Over the years I have accumulated a vast collection of clubs – about twelve bags' worth. The great majority just lurk in the cellar where I store them. They are only there because I have a daft habit of never trading-in. Don't ask me why. Out of that vast pile of clubs, I have just two drivers that I am really comfortable with; three putters, and an old wedge that it would really grieve me to lose. The rest are ballast.

Gadget man
One man who takes an opposite line on clubs is my good friend Sean Connery. There are two quite different reasons for this. The first is that he is one of the great putter-breakers. He plays his golf off a short fuse – as a lot of us

do – and when he explodes on the green his putter can say its prayers, because the odds are that he will snap it across his knee. Many is the round he has had to finish with a blade on a stick reduced to eighteen inches long. But even that is preferable – from his point of view – to the time we refused to give him a 2½-foot putt. He hit it, missed, snarled, gritted his teeth, took the putter in both hands, jerked it down over his knee – the usual routine – but this time it didn't break! Not only that, the impact did his leg in and he had to hobble off for treatment. (Isn't it strange how that kind of accident always gets a laugh?)

The second reason is that Sean is more inclined than I am to listen to scientific explanations. He likes all that gadget talk, and is not above using it himself to demoralize an opponent.

We were playing on the Las Brisas course in Spain. We had reached a difficult par five which, unless you are a mighty hitter and go straight for the green, is best played with some caution, e.g. a drive, a 5-iron into the corner, then a wedge to the green across a broad stretch of lake.

'Look at this, boy!'

Sean now drew from his bag a most beautiful club. He explained to me that this was a Ben Hogan double-duty wedge. He waggled it about impressively.

'I can play tunes on this,' he said. 'Had it over from America.' Waggle waggle. 'It's all there, boy.'

'Marvellous,' I breathed.

We played the hole. Sean drilled a lovely drive, then hit a firm 5-iron down to the corner. The next shot was ideal for the Ben Hogan double-duty wedge.

Sean struck it well, but . . . plop! The ball landed in the middle of the lake.

He took another ball. Plop! Into the lake.

Sean was boiling by now, but had not quite burst. He called to his caddie for a third ball. It performed the same parabola. Plop! Straight into the lake . . . followed almost immediately by the Ben Hogan double-duty wedge, which went in with an almighty splash.

Sean turned and glowered at his caddie. 'Now go and get that.'

'Maldito sea, vete y cogelo tu mismo,' said the caddie, and stood his ground.* Connery steamed in silent fury.

Sean, to give him credit, has never forgotten the incident.

*For a translation, buy a Spanish dictionary!

Although it happened seven years ago, I can still go round that course with him, and when we get to the big water hole, I say:

'Isn't that the one where . . . ?'

'Yes,' he replies crisply, looking straight ahead, apparently at something on the horizon. 'The double-duty wedge. It's still in there.'

Fore!

Violence is never far from the surface in golf. It is hardly surprising when you consider that the hitting instruments are very similar to the war hammers and maces that the mounted knights of old used to swing at each other. You might say that their game was a kind of 'golf on the gallop', with human heads for targets instead of Dunlop 65s.

Many of the people gathered at the prosperous Jewish golf club one sunny July day had no idea of the game's murderous side. They had come with their families to see a big pro-am event being staged there, and milled about all over the course.

Mayhem was inevitable. Sure enough, up on the tee, a member cracked a low drive which flew straight for an old Jewish spectator wandering in the fairway, struck him squarely on the back of the head and knocked him out. When he came round, he not only had an aching head, he was very angry with the golfer.

'Oh, oh, my head,' he moaned, then squinted up at the golfer, one hand clutching his throbbing dome. 'As for you, I'm going to sue you. I'm going to sue you for ten thousand pounds!'

'I shouted "Fore",' protested the golfer.

'I'll take it!' said the old boy.

THE SAYINGS OF DENIS

Denis: 'Do you know, I got on the green at the 4th in two!'

A Friend: 'Oh, well played. What did you make?'

Denis: 'Six.'

THE AVERAGE COMMITTEE MEMBER'S KNOWLEDGE OF GOLF

FURTHER USES OF A GOLF COURSE

You must have seen them – from a distance anyway. A strange face peering out of the woods beside the fairway; a blur of bright cloth behind a patch of bracken, followed by the sound of running feet. Who could have owned that old army boot you found in the rough? How did it get there?

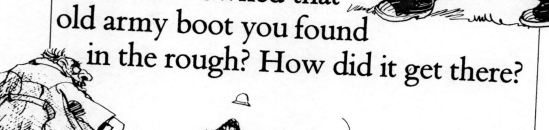

Golf courses in summer make marvellous refuges for all kinds of strangers who have no business being there – secret agents, defrocked accountants, tramps – or are they retired caddies of the old school, sleeping out their last summers? One lady member at our club sliced her tee shot into the trees, followed it in and met a masked flasher holding a golf ball in his hand.

'Here you are, lady,' offered the flasher.

She was very upset and later complained long and loud to the club secretary.

'Of course we will do everything we can to catch this dreadful man,' said the secretary. 'But tell me, have *you* any idea who it could have been?'

'Well,' said the affronted lady, 'I am quite certain he wasn't a member!'

Schoolboys find many uses for golf courses. There is always a choice of routes home from school, some taking up to an hour longer than others, but few can equal the golf course for opportunities: the thrill of duffing up a rare butterfly, or the quiet satisfaction of cornering the market in conkers – or the SAS/Action Man excitement, which no computer game can match, of being chased by a red-faced angry greenkeeper and getting clean away. Best of all is the sport of nicking golf balls that are still in play – or their owners think they still are. They thrash with their clubs at gorse bushes which conceal not just the golf ball, but the crouching breathless schoolboy in whose trouser pocket the golf ball is now lying. In forty-eight hours or less, that ball will be sold back to the club professional, who understands these things.

Some of these under-age invaders are getting so bold, you almost wonder who is the club member and who is the trespasser. In that long hot summer of 1976, when the golf courses had all turned brown from lack of rain and the heat of the sun, I was playing a fourball at Parkstone in Dorset, partnered by my good friend Gordon Dean. We had hit our drives at the 1st, and they had all gone bounding extra-long distances up the fairway on the bone-hard ground. We were walking up, when suddenly we heard a strange sound. Swish-whoosh. Swish-whoosh.

We looked round. Coming towards us along the fairway was a boy on roller skates! Gliding along he was, just like they do on seaside promenades. We thought to ourselves: we'll give him swish-whoosh. Someone shouted:

'Oi! Where the hell do you think you're going?'

The boy skated over and drew up alongside us. He said, very simply: 'Mam sent me out to find Dad. She said: "He's not playing golf all the bloody holiday."'

We let him through. What else could we do? We also had a good laugh at our vision of an infuriated Mum stuck in some boarding-house in Poole, giving instructions to the poor lad caught in the family crossfire: 'Go and find yer father. And don't come back until you've brought him with you!'

49

Poor old boy. The Dad, I mean. He probably thought he'd be doing everyone a favour if he crept off for an hour or two and played a few holes. Is that so wrong? I mean, there's wife evasion and there's wife evasion. All I can think is, she must have loved him very much to send out the cavalry to find him and drag him back!

Is that your member?

A couple I met one day on the golf course were showing no reservations at all about being together. They had found themselves a gently sloping uphill lie just over a mound by the 5th green, and were getting to an advanced stage of love-making when along I came with my friend the Brigadier.

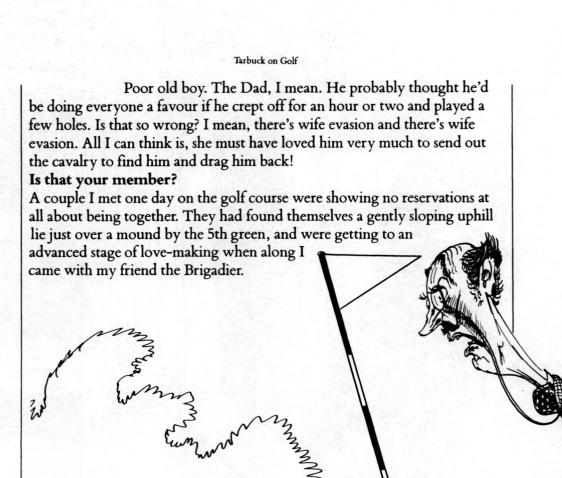

The Brigadier was also at that time the club secretary. As soon as we spotted the couple, I thought I would step back a pace or two and let the Brigadier handle the matter – as he clearly was not going to pass by on the other side without making some fairly forceful comment. Determined not to let the club down, he strode to the top of the mound, glared down at the couple through his monocle and barked:

'Are you members?'

Although, looking back, I consider that remark one of the

great statements of the twentieth century, at the time it was only a qualified success. Down on the grass, the male partner was very upset at being put off his stroke by some daft bloody golfer, and he replied with a fusillade of 'Piss off, mind your own damn business,' etc, etc. Later, after the Brigadier and I had driven off and were walking up the fairway, I said to him softly:

'"Are you members?" Did you really say that?'

The Brigadier looked, for him, more than a touch perplexed.

'Well,' he said, and his eyebrows shot up in a great heave of frustration, 'it was all I could think of!'

The new secretary

My friend the Brigadier was at the centre of another episode involving a 'stranger'. We were playing at St George's Hill, Weybridge, away from our own club, Coombe Hill, where the Brigadier was the secretary. We had finished our game and gone into the clubhouse. A few moments earlier, I had noticed the brewery drayman unloading a fresh delivery of crates and barrels and taking them into the club cellar. It was a warm day and, once he had done his work, someone must have offered him a glass, which he accepted. He came and sat up at the bar and began sipping at his glass of beer.

I turned to the Brigadier, motioned to the man and said: 'Have you met their new secretary?'

'No, I haven't,' said the Brigadier, his eyes immediately alight with interest. 'I must go and introduce myself.'

There is a great solidarity among club secretaries, and the Brigadier was in any case a great one for observing the correct form. He stood up, a tribute to his military rank with his neat white moustache, monocle and plus fours, and stepped briskly over to the drayman at the bar.

'How are you?' said the Brigadier, and announced himself: 'Davenport, Coombe Hill.'

'Owjerdo,' replied the drayman without much interest, and took another pull on his beer.

The Brigadier persisted. 'Do you like it here?' he asked.

'Not bad,' said the drayman.

'Ah,' said the Brigadier. 'Really? That's most interesting.'

He looked a bit nonplussed and gave a small glance round to where I was sitting, as though to signal that the conversation was not going brilliantly. However, he decided to give it another go, and said:

'Will you be at the secretaries' meeting at Walton Heath on the 27th?'

In a fruity Cockney voice the other man said: 'What the bleedin' 'ell would I be doin' that for?'

'Oh,' said the Brigadier, ever so slightly flustered, 'well, I, er, er . . .'

By now I was shaking with laughter; it was all I could do to keep the tears from plopping into my glass.

The Brigadier came over and sat down opposite me. He leaned forward and said, keeping his voice carefully lowered: 'You are naughty, Jimmy. You know, you really are . . . naughty!'

Animal capers

Then there is the wild life. What could be more pleasing, at the close of the day, with purple shadows lengthening, than to watch a deer trot with her fawn slowly across the fairway in the fading sunlight, as once happened to me at Gleneagles? A lovely sight. I am, in any case, a lover of evening golf; the game could have been invented for playing on calm, fine evenings when the busy world has stopped and you can gently unwind as you concentrate on your shots, clipping them through the still air, the tension oozing out of your body.

Not all animals, on the other hand, are quite so scenic, or so docile. I am thinking, in particular, of the snakes in Spain.

Once I was playing in a tournament at Atalaya Park with Oscar Struber and Sean Connery. While we were in the changing rooms Oscar – a portly gentleman who that day was wearing a pair of huge baggy shorts – decided he had better have a spell on the throne before we went out. So, while Sean and I put on our boots, Oscar went into the toilet and shut the door.

About a quarter of a minute later, the toilet door burst open and Oscar came whizzing out as though he had been fired from a gun. It turned out that a small snake had crawled up the porcelain between his legs, even as he was lowering himself onto the seat. The effect on Oscar was more rapid than syrup of figs – though the manner of the treatment was not at all to his liking!

007 strikes again

At Guadalmina I was again playing with Sean Connery. As we walked past a clump of rocks, suddenly a snake raised its head and hissed at us. Connery was superb. A quick backhander with his putter stunned it, then he followed up with three lightning chops just below the creature's head. Before the snake could recover, Connery dived in again. The air was blue with Scottish

oaths as the putter cracked down and down and down again on the snake, until there was not a twitch left in it. Leaving the broken animal on the rock, Connery resumed his march to the next green.

Only when he reached the green did he notice the damage he had inflicted on his putter, which now looked rather like a rendering in metal of the dead snake. More Scottish oaths.

Then, of course, he wanted to borrow someone else's putter to finish the hole. 'No!' we all cried, and looked on with great delight as Sean was forced to putt out with his own misshapen stick. Scottish oaths, Part 3.

Thorn bushes, incidentally, can be as bad as snakes. A prominent member of our club duffed one at the 3rd, and it went into a clump of thorns. The caddie said he thought he could play it, so the member groped his way inside and eventually knocked the ball out.

When he emerged he said to the caddie: 'Where's it gone?'

The caddie said: 'Who are you?'

The member swung round, and saw to his horror that his wig had detached itself and was hanging daintily from a thorn branch.

So, if you wear one, beware. It could happen to you.

Rex

Beware, also, the bloke who wants to bring his dog round with him. They can be very distracting. I was over at Sunningdale when a toff came up. Plus-fours, matching sweater, cap at a jaunty angle. By his feet, a Jack Russell.

'Do you mind if Rex and I join you?' said the toff.

'Please do,' we said.

The toff hit his first shot, 140 yards down the middle, not a bad effort. Immediately, the dog sat up on its haunches, put its two front paws together in a clapping motion and barked:

'Woof-woof. Woof-woof.'

Then he ran round his master's feet in little circles.

The same thing happened after the second shot. And when his master sank his putt, little Rex nearly went berserk with delight.

I said to the toff: 'What happens if you miss a putt, or knock one out of bounds?'

'Oh,' he said, 'Rex does somersaults.'

'Really,' I said, 'how many does he do?'

'It all depends,' said the toff, 'on how hard I kick him up the arse.'

THE SAYINGS OF DENIS

Denis: 'Will you look at that!'

A Friend: 'Where are you, Denis?'

Denis: 'At the bottom of that pine tree.'

A Friend: 'What's so great about that?'

Denis: 'If I'd cleared that tree, I'd be on the green!'

SUNSHINE GOLF

The umbrella is a wonderful invention. At the press of a button, in theory, a metal palm tree of spokes suddenly flies up the shaft and a big round canopy spreads out over your head. This, you can almost guarantee, will keep you safe – well, from the knees up – from every kind of terrible weather known to man. There are sun umbrellas, too, and golf umbrellas.

No umbrella, however, could have solved the problems of the old member at Royal Ashdown Forest. It was during the great heatwave of '76, and the course was plagued by flies to such an extent that the members were having great difficulty playing their shots. The flies swarmed everywhere, swooped under the umbrellas, perched on the members' heads, bit them . . .

George Hammond, one of the organizers of the Suntory and many other great tournaments, and a confirmed golf nut, was invited down to the club's Open Day and found himself drawn with this old gentleman. As they stood on the 1st tee the old fellow pulled out two pieces of pole from his bag. One had a metal connecting piece at the end and they looked as if they might once have had something to do with a large tent, or a chimney sweep. When he had joined the two poles together, the old member said with some confidence to George:

'We won't be troubled by flies today.'

While George stood and boggled, the old member then drew from another compartment of his golf bag . . . a kipper. He fixed it on top of the pole, and then he and George played their eighteen holes. Each time it was one man's turn to play, the other stood behind him and held the pole with the kipper over his head. The flies were no trouble at all. They were all up in the air, savaging the kipper.

Steam heat

Spain, Portugal, and more recently Tunisia have become the new centres for holiday golf. I thoroughly approve, even though I sometimes feel that certain courses are getting overcrowded, leading to impossibly long rounds and other problems which I discuss later in this chapter.

In Britain we are caught in a weather trap. From April or May, and onwards through the summer, our golf courses are the finest in the world *and* a great pleasure to visit and play. In January or February, though, it is no picnic up on the Ayrshire coast, or anywhere else when snow is on the ground and your hands have turned blue and rigid before you get to the second tee. Whereas, in just two and a half hours you can nip down from London to the Costa del Sol or the Algarve, where they have a beautiful climate in the early part of the year, and also some of the most marvellous golf courses you will find anywhere.

Which are my favourites? Well, in no particular order, you could try Vilamoura, Quinta do Lago, Estoril, Penina, Palmares, Vale do Lobo – the whole of the Algarve is a golfing paradise. In Spain there is the Las Brisas course in Marbella, and if I had to make do with one course for all time, the Old Course at Sotogrande would do me very well.

The first time I went on a golfing holiday to Spain I was with a bunch of pals – Kenny Lynch was there, also Del Simmons the snooker organizer. It was about fifteen years ago and we chose Marbella. In those days it was not the Marbella you see now: the famous marina at Puerto Banus did not exist, and in fact the whole of the Costa del Sol has since been transformed.

The most memorable incident of that first trip to the sun took place off the course. In a sauna, to be precise. Our hired car had been involved in a slight accident, and the next day the hire company sent its representative round to our hotel. We were all in the sauna when he arrived. Very smart in his company outfit he was, with the blazer, trousers, shirt, tie all matching and toning with each other. His cuffs, I remember, looked supremely crisp and immaculate as he appeared in the doorway of the sauna.

'I have the form for you to sign, señor,' he announced.

'Come in, come in,' we said, and manoeuvred him inside and shut the door. Del Simmons, who is a big lad, stood in front of the door while the Spanish representative tried to get someone to sign his form, only to be met with strange delaying tactics and stubborn questioning. 'Yes, but what is this bit here?' 'What does that mean?' 'Why is paragraph 2(a) longer than the others?' And on and on while the temperature inside the sauna had the poor man tugging at his collar ('Is *muy* hot here, señor'), and the sweat poured down his face.

Best of all was the rapid collapse of his company uniform. As the outfit turned wringing wet before our eyes, the creases vanished, the starch melted and his trousers, shirt cuffs and blazer sleeves began to shrink. All over his body items of clothing were beating a desperate retreat. In the end we let him do the same. I won't tell you the name of the company, but he didn't try so hard for the rest of that day.

After that, garment shrinking became an art form. Another member of our party was Jack Siegler, a most careful and immaculate dresser. Proudly he told me about a new pair of beautiful lemon slacks which he planned to wear when we went out the next evening.

In the morning I was passing the open door of his room. I looked inside and saw the maid taking the sheets off Jack's bed. Over the back of a chair hung the beautiful, virginal lemon slacks.

'Buenos dias,' I said to the maid, stepping inside. 'Are you doing some washing today? Lavar?' I made rubbing gestures between clenched fists. The maid nodded. I pointed to the lemon slacks and said: 'Just give those a rinse through, will you?'

'Si, señor,' she said.

In no time she had the slacks washed and hung up to dry. Out in the garden Jack was laughing and joking with the rest of us. The day ticked merrily by. We even played some golf. When the time came to go out Jack went to his room, came out and said:

'Have you seen those new slacks of mine?'

I said: 'Where did you leave them?'

He said: 'Over the chair.'

'Oh,' I said, 'you want to be very careful of the maids here. They'll wash anything they find left out.'

Jack dashed off in a blur of light. Too late. The maid had

60

ironed the lemon slacks. It is hardly an exaggeration to say that when Jack put them on they came about halfway up to his knees. Well, *we* thought it was funny.

French leave

Fifteen years on, the exodus from Northern Europe has threatened to become a flood. The main drawback to this is that the standard of golf played on the Costa del Sol is not what it used to be, and you can get stuck for hours behind great blocks of near-total novices. Sometimes four of them go round with one bag between them, and wander hither and thither for the rest of the day.

As a race, the French are not noted for their golfing prowess, and when I saw this vast group from the Club Méditerranée ahead of us, about forty of them, I knew that drastic steps were called for. We had arrived at the course a few minutes late, and the Club people were on the tee. I ran down to them.

'Mesdames, messieurs!' I cried to them. 'Attention!' I apologized for my poor French and said I would speak to them in English. 'Welcome,' I went on, 'I am so pleased that you are all going to play in the Secretary's Cup competition.'

'Compétition?' said their leader. 'I did not know there was a compétition.'

'Yes, yes,' I cried. 'We are putting it up specially for the Club Méditerranée. It's a beautiful trophy, and the winner gets a free week's holiday.'

The French gabbled noisily amongst themselves, with lots of gestures and shoulder-heaving. 'Oliday? Coupe Secrétaire? Vacances gratuites? Oh, bravo!'

They seemed to be buying it. 'Now, mesdames, messieurs,' I continued, 'for this competition the tee is the other way from

61

the clubhouse. What you must do is go back there, get your cards and the club officials will tell you exactly what to do.'

'Oh, sank you, monsieur', cried the leader. 'Bravo.' He translated my words to the others and soon the whole party was trooping back towards the clubhouse.

'Right,' I said to my mates who had advanced cautiously towards the tee, bringing their clubs and mine. 'Let's go.'

We drove off quickly. The 1st is a long par five and we were well down the fairway, playing our second shots, when the agonized shouting reached us.

'Monsieur!' the leader was yelling at the top of his voice. 'Mon-si-eur!'

'Oui, oui,' I yelled back, scribbling in the air on an imaginary card. 'Compétition! Very good!'

It may not have been the height of etiquette, but in the final reckoning my small deception could never have been in the same league of pain as the agony that French crowd would have inflicted on us if we had

stayed behind them. To go further, I would say there is a moral to be gained from that experience.

The moral is, if you go golfing in Spain, go organized. There are now specialist travel companies who set up golfing holidays in the sun, and they can save the average traveller a great deal of hassle. I have seen many instances where parties of, say, four friends make all their own bookings, go to Spain, only to find when they get there that it is very hard, and sometimes impossible, to get on the more famous courses, which naturally are the ones they had set their hearts on playing.

Whereas, if you go with an expert holiday firm (Eurogolf, Benagolf and Longshot are three that come to mind) they have the tees booked in advance. They block-book for their own private tournaments, and you can plan your days without having to worry. The night before, you can look up your starting time on the notice board in the hotel. If it says that Tarbuck, Hopkins and Parsons are due off at 11.10, that's all you need to know. You can then arrange to get there in comfort and have time to hit some practice shots. You will also have a good idea when you will finish, so you can fix up your evening. No stress, no panic; it must be a better way.

Over here, Parkie

The incident with the French party reminds me that sunny Spain was also the venue for another unexpected change of direction. This so impressed the unfortunate victim that he wrote about it in his column in *The Sunday Times*.

Michael Parkinson (for it was he) is a fairly recent convert to golf. In fact, he used to be president of the Anti-Golf Society, which he founded as a way of getting back at his mates who were always out on the golf course when he wanted to see them.

He still finds the game quite difficult, and I was not surprised to hear his reaction when I pointed out to him that his next shot was eighty yards up to a green heavily guarded by a screen of pine trees and bushes.

'Jesus Christ!' said Parkie. 'That's impossible.'

Just then a Spanish greenkeeper working on the green spotted us and started shouting and waving his arms. He was too far off for us to be able to pick out his actual words. I said to Parkie:

'Take no notice of him. What does he know anyway, miserable Iberian.' Or words to that effect.

So Parkie played his shot. He seemed quite pleased with it. The hole, however, was the other way.

'Not too bad,' he said to me, with a bit of a gleam in his eye.

'No', I said. 'But your next shot will be interesting. The flag's down there.' I pointed in the opposite direction, and burst out laughing.

'You rotten ———!' said Parkie. 'No wonder you wanted that greenkeeper to mind his own business.'

He trudged off into the distance, towards the torrent of Spanish and fractured English now coming from the greenkeeper. 'I tell you, señor. I tell you. But you no listen.'

'Ah, shurrup!'

Michael's big friend

Michael was also in our party when Sean Connery and I were challenged by a Leeds United team who were down on the Costa del Sol. We agreed a stake, and the Leeds boys picked Eddie Gray and Norman Hunter to win it for them.

Sean has the unique asset of a dual identity. When people meet him for the first time, you can see in their faces that they are looking at, and speaking to, James Bond, rather than the actor who played him. It is not at all a bad image to have at your disposal, as we shall see. Sean has also perfected a set of put-downs designed to throw people off their golf. Phrases such as 'Where did you get your handicap, the Coop?' can be quite devastating to a first-timer.

The Leeds boys, with their background in professional sport, managed to weather these insults – even if they were a little bit distracted by the presence of 007 – and we reached the turn all square. Now we were playing down the side of the course, which was bordered by a row of gardens attached to holiday villas, with just a low hedge separating the villas from the golf course.

We had quite a little crowd following us round, and one observant member of the group noticed that there were some women sunbathing in one of the gardens. So now everyone was walking down the fairway with his head screwed at right-angles to the direction of his body. Then Sean went up to the hedge and looked over. As Ian Fleming might have put it: 'Bond's eyes were warm azure pools.'

'Hello,' he said softly. 'Hello'.

The women all stood up. 'Ach,' they cried, 'Chems Bondt!' (They were Germans.) They were also topless – and impressively well put-together. Soon they were trotting out on the golf course.

'Hello, boys!'

'Hello, girls!'

The golf was forgotten in the sudden rush to say hello to these bronzed and friendly German ladies. Eventually one of them said:

'You will come and have drinks. After?'

'Yes! Yes!'

Back, urgently, to the golf. Having torn ourselves away from the ladies, we played the next seven holes at 80 mph. Putts were given all round. 'Yes, yes, that's a gimme. Of course it is. Come on!' We got to the 18th, finished the round, and were sprinting up the hill to the clubhouse when who should we meet but another group of ladies, including my wife Pauline and Parkie's wife Mary, who were out having a drink on the verandah.

Dropping quickly to a casual saunter, we approached our lawful wedded ladies and I said to my wife:

'I've been thinking. Have we got any lagers back at the villa? If not, could you get some at the supermarket and we'll follow you down when we've changed.'

Pretty smart, eh? The wives rose to leave, and we let them get round the corner, then sprinted for our cars and hurtled off to our rendezvous. We reached a roundabout just near the German ladies' villa, when one of our hostesses-to-be, still massively topless, came out on to the balcony overlooking the road and waved to us.

'Hello, boys!'

'Hello!' we all called back. 'Hello!'

Just then, from the other direction, a familiar car approached. In it was the other group of ladies, i.e. my wife, Parkie's wife, etc.

'Jesus!' We shot off as fast as we could back to our villa, and managed to get home before our wives. Later, we were out in the garden when Pauline said to me:

'Who was that you were talking to?'

'Oh,' I said. 'Big friend of Michael.'

THE SAYINGS OF DENIS

It is not just raining, it is teeming down and a thunderstorm has just started. Members watch from the clubhouse window as the lightning forks into the fairway.

Denis: 'What's the weather forecast?'

A Friend: 'Rain all day.'

Denis: 'This'll go off in a minute.'

THE PROFESSORS

In every man's life there are a handful of people he will never forget. His parents; the teacher who gave him the hardest time at school; the first girl who didn't say no; his wife and children; and the golf pro who gave him his first lessons, a handicap, and a purpose in life.

It is such a highly personal choice that everyone wants to rate *their* golf pro as the rudest, gentlest, most savage, most domineering and quietly charming person who ever drew breath. I will not dispute that. They are all different. And yet, in my novice days, a golf pro was very much a certain kind of man, with a certain set of characteristics that he shared only with other golf pros.

For a start, his life centred on his club, to which he was bound by obscure feudal laws. There were no tournament pros then, and the club pro was not forever nipping off to distant parts to compete for trunkloads of dollars. A few times a year, perhaps, he would set off somewhere in his battered motor car (and usually the prize money barely covered his expenses). The rest of the time, he was where the committee liked him best – in his shop or out on the course, playing and teaching, and giving the members the rough edge of his tongue, for which they loved him.

'Dick, I'd like to hit it further.'

'Hit it effing harder, then!'

'Oh! I see. Thank you, Dick.'

That was Dick Burton, my own mentor at Coombe Hill

69

(talking to someone else, by the way). Dick, who won the 1939 Open, was maybe the unluckiest champion of all because the war then took six years out of his career when he was at his peak. In an earlier chapter ('Why Golf?') I explained how passionately Dick liked to win. He brought bite and a sense of urgency into everything he did at Coombe Hill. He also thought his time was precious, and resented any member who tried to put it to what he thought was unprofitable use.

One day I went up to the 1st tee, and Dick came striding along. You could recognize Dick from quite some way off because he always gave lessons in his overcoat. Here he came, his overcoat clipping the wind, followed by an agitated-looking member who was having to trot to keep within range of him.

'Dick!' the member was calling out in a plaintive kind of way. 'Come back.'

'No, sir!' said Dick firmly, and carried on walking rapidly away from the member.

'But Dick . . .'

'No, sir! You're wasting my effing time and your effing money!'

The poor chap was never seen again.

King Arthur

At Sunningdale there was little doubt who ruled the roost. Arthur Lees. A portrait of him hangs in state in the clubhouse, matched only by another of Jimmy Sheridan, the great caddiemaster of former times.

Arthur was another of the select band who had a shrewd idea both of his value to the club and what he could make of it. Members who tried to procure his services for less were asking for a sharp reminder – and usually got it.

I was in the club bar once, and to my surprise Cecil Elliott, one of the great watchers of the game at Sunningdale, had not come up and given me his usual warm greeting: 'You here again?'

I was still recovering from this when Arthur came in. Another member, who had been waiting for him, got up and said:

'Right, Arthur. Are you ready, then?'

'Aye,' said Arthur in his unruffled Yorkshire voice. 'Aye. Let's get out to the tee.'

'I'll tell you what, Arthur,' said the member as they went out. 'I'll play you for ten pounds and automatic presses.'

Arthur's jaw dropped. 'Ten pound?' he said. 'Ten pound?' It sounded as if he had never heard of such a figure. 'I'll tell you what, mister,' he went on, 'I'm not goin' out theer for ten pound.'

The member was taken aback but soon recovered. 'Look here, Arthur. It seems to me you'd sooner have our money than our company.'

Arthur looked him square in the eye. 'Too bloody true I would. Too bloody true!'

They settled for twenty.

Nor was there much wrong with Arthur's memory. When it came to recalling great shots he had played, he also had that special gift of making them *sound* like the world-beaters they very often were.

'Eeeh, mister. I had this fifteen-footer. And the green went off right . . . then it come back left. For three hundred pound it were, mister. So I looked at it . . . then I hit it. Oh dear, dear. I only *just* got it in.'

Arthur was one of the great professors of golf. He could sum up a man's entire game in seconds. And then the treatment would begin.

'Oh, nooo, no. Nooo, no. Yer can't play with clubs like those.'

There followed a brief interval while  he took the member back to his shop and fitted him up with a new set. Then out they went on the course again, where Arthur could be the most patient and saintly teacher, chipping and putting with his pupils for hours, advising, cajoling, geeing them along.

As well as humble club members by the score, many a mighty professional had reason to thank Arthur for his help and tuition. Wayne Player, son of the great Gary, was once in the practice bunker at Sunningdale. Arthur watched him for a bit and then ambled over.

'Nooo, no,' he said. 'Look, lad. Stand a bit more this way. Get yer 'and round it like that . . .'

Wayne Player was not delighted. 'Mr Lees,' he said firmly, 'I must point out to you that I have been taught by the greatest bunker player in the world. My father, Gary Player.'

Arthur said: 'Yer daft booger. Who d'yer think taught him?'

The Laird of Woburn

'He is a very competitive player . . . his action is very basic with only a three-quarter length backswing, from which a good deal of shoulder work and gritting of the teeth is required to make the ball fly as it might from a freer action . . .'

The writer is Alex Hay, long-time friend, BBC commentator and professional at Woburn Golf and Country Club, and he is giving his views on my swing for *Golf Illustrated*. I'm not so keen on that section of his report, as a matter of fact, but later I felt his accuracy began to improve:

'. . . the posture is very good and he maintains the angle of his spine throughout the action . . . because of the retention of good angle the plane of the swing is excellent . . .'

And so on. Good reliable stuff from there on. Mind you, he would not have wanted to be over-critical. Not after all the generous things I said about him at Ferndown during last year's Hennessy Cup.

Alex arrived there to join the BBC commentary team, just when it was becoming apparent to the organizers that there had been a mix-up over the invitations, and Brian Barnes was not going to turn up for the pro-am tournament preceding the main event. Alex suddenly found himself dragooned into the Scotland team for the pro-am, and was told: 'You're next on the tee.'

Fortunately the news reached me just in time. Alex was all for sneaking off from the 1st tee unannounced. For one thing, he didn't know the course; for another, he had to borrow his clubs and kit from the Assistant Pro. He might have succeeded if his borrowed gear hadn't been so uncomfortable that he was still struggling with his glove and worrying about the thickness of the grip on his driver . . . when I managed to reach a microphone. Alex himself has described the next few seconds:

'I got myself set, said a short prayer, and then it happened. From the loudspeakers: "Representing Scotland, Woburn, and the BBC, and using borrowed clubs, Alex Hay, the Laird of Woburn." I tried to pretend I didn't hear this and started my backswing. "He'll be takkin' the club back verra slow and turrnin' frae the troosers up!"

'Finally I had to play and I hit the biggest slice ever; away it soared into the forest. "Aye, he'll feel at hame in thair."'

A couple of days later, during the three-way tournament between Great Britain, Rest of the World and Europe, Alex started warbling on in his commentary about the 1st hole at Ferndown and how marvellous it was, what a fine test of golf, etcetera. I reached for the phone.

In the BBC production caravan at Ferndown someone took my call. A message was passed through to Alex: 'Tarbuck would like to know how you are such an authority on the 1st hole, considering you've never been on it!'

THE SAYINGS OF DENIS

Denis: 'That bloody caddy! He put me off.'
A Friend: 'Oh? What did he do?'
Denis: 'I don't know. He just put me off.'

DENTED GROUSE, AND OTHER MISHAPS

By day we marched through the rainswept valleys of the King's Course, did battle with Broomy Law, Whaup's Nest, Braid's Brawest and the others, cheered on our way – or should that be jeered? – by passing flocks of wild geese, grouse and pheasant. By night there was a temptation really to let go, and enjoy all the facilities of Scotland's only five-star hotel.

One evening during the Pro-Celeb week at Gleneagles, a group of us were in the bar. Sir Ian Stewart, the Scottish industrialist, was there; also Sean Connery, Michael Medwin and some others. We had one or two tots; then – it had been a cold day out on the course – we had a few more. Time passed. A good evening began to take shape.

Out in the foyer of the hotel stands a very fine tableau showing a Highland still, with typical Highland scenery and running water. Several stuffed grouse complete the scene. As we sat round in the bar an idea began to form in my mind. I went out to the foyer, took two of the grouse off the tableau, and brought them back to the bar. The grouse were to be the stars of an intimate puppet show I planned to give. I got down behind a table, like a Punch and Judy man, and let the birds take over.

They were soon at it. 'Hello, little girl.' 'Get lost!' 'Oooh!'

The show went down very well with the audience. Parts of it were robust if not rude, and what with the birds nipping each other in the tail feathers as they grew more and more excited, and then one mounting the other . . . a certain amount of damage was inevitable. First a wing fell off the

male lead, then his mate was suddenly headless; stuffing poured onto the hotel carpet from both birds.

When at last the performance was consummated, it was time for everyone to go to bed. This left me, at three o'clock in the morning, standing in the bar holding two very scrawny animals. I went out to the foyer, tossed them back on the Highland Scene and went upstairs.

Next morning came too soon for me, but duty called. I had to be on the tee at nine o'clock. I took a shower, which helped a little, then cut myself shaving and bled so much that my eyes cleared. Feeling only halfway healthy I stepped out of the lift on the ground floor . . . and there was the hotel manager, Mr James Bannatyne OBE. He looked at me sternly.

'Good morning, Mr Tarbuck,' he said. 'Good morning to *you*, Mr Bannatyne,' I replied, and moved off smartly.

I had gone about four paces when the austere voice of the manager called after me: 'I believe we bagged a brace last night?'

'Hmm, yes,' I mumbled, adding a pair of politely rapped knuckles to my other injuries, and retreated in search of strong coffee.

Sandwich man

Bruce Forsyth had been having a hard time with the autograph-hunters. Or so he claimed. He was at the Open, sharing a house with Ian Brill and Kenny Lynch.

'I'm fed up with them, luv,' he complained one morning. 'They're all after me. I can't watch the golf.'

It is true that autograph-hunters can be a bit like locusts at a big event such as the Open, and too often show little sympathy for their victim. Anyway, Bruce had had enough. He was going to disguise himself.

He put on a false moustache (not over his real one, this was before he had a real one), dark glasses, a hat, and a big raincoat. 'No-one will recognize me now,' he said to Kenny. 'No,' said Kenny, and off they went to the golf.

When they reached the course, Bruce strode ahead and Kenny pulled out an envelope on which he had written 'This is Bruce Forsyth'. When the right moment came, he gently stuck it on the back of Bruce's raincoat.

All afternoon the fans kept coming up to Bruce and asking for his autograph.

'I can't understand it,' whiffled poor Bruce to Kenny through his stick-on tash. 'They keep recognizing me!'

'I think they can tell who you are,' said Kenny, ever helpful.

Rake's progress

It may not be as widely known as he would like it to be, but Bruce is the unluckiest golfer in the world. If you ask him, he will tell you.

'The luck I'm having, luv. Oh dear. You wouldn't believe it!'

We tell him he shouldn't moan so much. At Sotogrande, we were going out for a fourball and the rest of us decided that we must be firm with Bruce.

'Now look,' we said. 'No moaning today. N-o m-o-a-n-i-n-g. Right?'

'All right,' said Bruce. 'I promise. I promise you I won't moan. I won't moan.'

We played the 1st hole and Bruce made a respectable par four. As we were walking across to the 2nd tee, he turned to us and said:

'I didn't moan. I didn't moan, did I?'

'No,' we agreed. 'Well done, Bruce. You didn't moan.'

The 2nd is a par five. Bruce played it gallantly, and spoke not a word until he had picked his ball out of the hole. Then he said:

'Well. That's two holes. Two holes and I haven't moaned.'

The 3rd at Sotogrande must count as an awkward little hole, a dog-leg left. We all drove off quite well, and from where his ball stopped Bruce needed a wedge or a 9-iron to reach the green. It's a clover-shaped green, well protected by bunkers, and the second shot to it is seldom easy.

Bruce hit a super shot that day. The weight was right, the direction was perfect, everything was super – until, halfway over the bunker, the ball hit the top of a rake which someone had left standing upright in the

78

sand. The ball dropped, stricken, into the bunker.

It was such an unbelievable piece of bad luck that the rest of us burst into instant hysterics. Bruce strode up to the bunker and glared down into it. Then he turned and wagged his finger at us.

'I'm not moaning,' he said. 'I'm not moaning. Mind you, I should bloody moan . . .'

Till Death?

Not all the celebrities who enjoy a game of golf are accident-prone. Johnny Speight, a nervous man at the best of times, with a pronounced stutter, prefers to live his life on the quiet side, and rarely gets into trouble. He was certainly less than overjoyed when someone at a pro-am event slipped him one of those exploding golf balls without mentioning the fact.

Johnny swung his driver. 'Boom!' went the golf ball. Johnny nearly had a heart attack.

'What the eff-eff-eff-eff-eff-effing hell was that?' he wanted to know. Quite right too.

Eric and the matches

Eric Sykes is unlikely to deny that he is hard of hearing. Not when he is always turning it so skilfully to his advantage. 'I know, I know,' he cries if he doesn't want to hear something, and moves away. 'Poor Eric,' people say, adding, 'he's deaf as a post, you know.'

One day Eric dropped a box of Swan Vestas on the green. Being hard of hearing, he didn't hear it fall, and walked on. I was playing in the following group with Glen Mason. Glen chipped up to the green and his ball ran smack into Eric's box of matches. A spectator explained what had happened and Glen bellowed up the course:

'Eric! Eric!'

Not a flicker from Eric.

'Eric! Eric!'

At last Eric must have heard something. He turned round.

'Eric!' bawled Glen. 'You've left a box of matches on the green, I've chipped up and my bloody ball's hit the box.'

Eric nodded and waved. 'Yes,' he said. 'I've got my four.' And walked on.

There is another story about Eric which he himself swears is true. If it is, then Eric is certainly enjoying the best of both of his worlds.

He was playing in a pro-am at Fulford Heath and was drawn with Isao Aoki, who doesn't speak much English. After they had both driven the 1st and were walking up, Eric said to Aoki:

'What did you think of my tee shot?'

Aoki stopped and bowed. 'Very good,' he said, 'but sleeves a little long.'

Underwater golf

One of the great golfing mishaps took place, I am proud to say, at my own club, Coombe Hill. The committee had decided to instal an underground watering system right round the course, on tees, greens and fairways. This was an adventurous move and Coombe Hill was one of the first British clubs to provide a system on this scale. It cost all the members £50 extra without the option, but in my view despite the odd grumbles about lack of consultation, etc, it was money well invested.

At last the day came for the water to be switched on. This great moment was arranged to coincide with the driving-in ceremony for the new club captain, which at Coombe Hill happens in the middle of the summer.

It was a beautiful day, and on the terrace outside the clubhouse every chair was taken, every table was filled with champagne glasses and Pimms, everyone was chatting away in high good humour. The ladies were present in strength, beautifully decked out in their best summer dresses; there were one or two elegant hats to be seen, sparkling hairdos, Gucci with everything.

The captain was all ready to drive in. Just before this happened, it had been agreed that the water on the 18th green would be turned on so that all the members and their friends could see precisely how it worked.

I had been playing shortly before, and as the time drew near for the brilliant cascade to make its appearance on the 18th, I went over to the locker-room window and looked out. I could see the whole perfect English scene spread out before me. As I stood there, the loudspeakers began to deliver one of those mangled streams of welcoming words without which an official occasion isn't official. '. . . jaast let you crackle whatya hiss pinngg's been spent on . . . great bleazzurre turn on zoingg put your drinks down now and we'll crackle cough splutter . . .'

The voice burbled on like this for another half minute or so and then we were given to expect that the button would be pressed and the magnificent new watering system would spring to life on the 18th green. All eyes turned in that direction. The button was pressed. To my intense joy, but not to anyone else's, it was the wrong button. Whoooshh!

Suddenly water was gushing up everywhere, through places where no-one even thought there were pipes. On the terrace, not a single spectator survived without a soaking. Best coiffures, dresses, hats, suits and shirts were saturated.

Angry voices could be heard in the button-pressing department. 'Don't you talk to me about how to do it!' 'You bloody idiot, what did you press that for?' 'I didn't.' 'Well, press it now.' 'It's not the right one, that's for the 6th tee.' 'Well, press it anyway.'

In the pandemonium and chaos the people in charge of the buttons were sending up jets of water all over the place. At every compass point on the course, sudden hisses and whooshes announced more fountains and yet more fountains. Meanwhile on the terrace it must have been like trying to balance on the deck of the *Titanic* wearing roller skates.

As organizational cock-ups go, this was one of the finest it has been my privilege to see. In the safety of the locker-room I screamed and screamed with laughter. To crown it all, the ceremony was followed by a dance. There was no time to go home, change, or dry hair which, seconds earlier, had been elegantly waved and lacquered, and now hung in distressed rat's tails. The dance must go on, and so it did. People knew their duty. Bedraggled but not beaten, they took to the floor and steamed around it until honour was satisfied. No-one at Coombe Hill who saw it will ever forget The Day They Turned The Water On.

GRAND TOUR

'Come over,' they said.

'Come over for the trip. It takes ten days.'

'Fine,' I said.

We were talking about the Bob Hope Classic, which was due to take place shortly. I went over, and was launched into the most fantastic round of American hospitality I have experienced. I went everywhere, was treated like a king, found I enjoyed it, stayed another night. 'Hey, can you play tomorrow?' 'I'll be there.' I stayed another night. So it went on.

Two days before the Hope tournament I was made an honorary member of the Tamarisk Golf and Country Club in Palm Springs, which was a joy; the kind of place where you casually bump into people like Frank Sinatra and Andy Williams in the bar.

Total opulence was in fact the hallmark of all the clubhouses I went to over there. Each was so fully and beautifully equipped, you could live in there for the rest of your life. You would want for nothing. Baths, showers, easy chairs, wonderful food – and that's just the locker-room.

83

Breakfast in a locker-room at Palm Springs is my idea of bliss. 'Will ya have a little cream cheese and bacon? French fries? Corn beef hash?' 'Thank you. I think I will . . .'

The way the Hope tournament is organized, the amateurs stay together in teams of three and are drawn with a different pro on each of the four days. On my first day I drew Jerry Pate; on the second it was Mr America himself, Arnold Palmer – or do I mean God? On the third day I played with Bobby Nicholls, and on the fourth with Hubert Green. A cream draw. It was purely a matter of luck, as was my good fortune in being drawn with two amateurs who were excellent company through the week.

An early highlight of the tournament came when Arnold Palmer scored a hole in one on the first day. I was on the next tee with Jerry Pate when a deafening roar went up that must have been clearly audible in Scotland Road, Liverpool. A few moments later we came across a steward who had missed all the excitement. In a slightly irritable way he asked us:

'What the hell was all that noise back there?'

'Arnold Palmer's just had a hole in one.'

The official, looking even more unimpressed, came out with a remark that must be a classic for a golf steward: 'Well, so he should. He plays often enough.'

Jerry Pate roared with laughter and the steward looked bleaker than ever. Back on the other green they were still yelling and whooping for King Arnie.

The Shed

I was walking round with Bob Hope at one stage in the week, when he sprang an unexpected invitation.

'Come up to the Shed,' he said.

'Yes, OK,' I said, not knowing what to expect.

I followed him up the side of a mountain, past security guards manning a pair of massive gates, and came upon the most astonishing house I have seen in my life – and I can claim to have seen a few fairly breathtaking houses. The Hope residence in Palm Springs has nearly two acres of roof, an Olympic swimming pool, and a par 3 golf hole with a waterfall beside it. The house has two wings, Hope explained, as he showed me round. He slept in Palm Springs; Dolores slept in Los Angeles.

We played a game of pool, and the Master patiently answered my questions while I bruised his ears about the art of comedy. He also had a few golf stories to tell. One was about Gerald Ford, whom I was later to meet and found entirely charming. Hope, however, was more than slightly scathing about Ford's mental equipment.

'There are something like twenty golf courses in Palm Springs,' said Hope. 'And Gerry Ford never knows which one he's on until he's hit his first shot!'

There was another problem you had to contend with when playing with American presidents. 'You are out there with Gerry Ford,' Hope explained, 'and the trees move down the fairway with you.'

Later, Hope confided to me: 'Jim, I could take six shots off your game' – he snapped his fingers – 'just like that.'

'Could you?' I said. 'How would you do that?'

Hope gave the famous smirk. 'Cut out one of the short holes.'

Going places

The trip to the Hope Classic was doubly significant for me because I was invited to take part in the huge gala which came at the end of the event. My act was well received, and, when Palm Springs was over, the invitations came rolling in. I was asked to play in the Andy Williams tournament and the Bing Crosby. Meanwhile I was staying in another fairly incredible home – the Tom Jones residence in Beverly Hills. It was a golden period. The hospitality I received was second to none.

First I went down to San Diego for the Andy Williams event. On the way I stopped at La Costa and played in a tournament there. Now I found myself running into American professionals I had known for many a year, people like Ben Crenshaw, and Jerry Pate again.

'Hey, Jim,' they'd say, surprised. 'What are you doing here?'

'Oh,' I'd reply. 'I've joined the circuit.'

It felt as though I almost had. People were coming up, ringing up, with golfing dates stretching into the following month. It was so easy to say yes. I went on saying yes until I received a call from my wife Pauline, in London.

'Come home,' she said.

It was a fair cop. I went.

THE INTRUDING EYE

It is not easy, at the best of times, to maintain a shining public image while performing in front of television cameras. It is far, far harder when the name of the game is golf. Playing under the eye of the camera must be one of the most unpredictable torments a man can submit to. However, when the reward for success is a beautiful 36-piece set of Waterford Crystal, a man must do what he can.

To make matters worse, on this particular occasion I thought I had the prize, awarded for the best amateur score, in my grasp. Coming to the last in the BBC2 Marley tournament at Gleneagles, I needed a birdie four to score nineteen points – and the crystal would be mine.

I ripped the drive in fine style and walked up. The lie was good. Easy 6-iron, I decided. I got ready to play my next shot and: Whoomph! The TV camera blew up.

We had to wait forty-five minutes before they could resume filming. By that time the adrenalin had stopped flowing, my back had stiffened up, and I couldn't decide which club to take. It didn't seem like a

6-iron any more. Was it a 5-iron? Perhaps a 4-iron?

Another thing I didn't know was that each day's play was piped live into the hotel lounge, where the guests could follow it on a big screen; beside the screen was a sign announcing who was currently going round, e.g. 'Trevino & Tarbuck v Ballesteros & Connery'.

Eventually the BBC crew were ready. The camera was lined up on my shot, and the sound man advanced with one of those great airships of a microphone, which are so sensitive that if anyone burps in the middle of Dundee you can hear it in Southend.

I tried to gee myself up with visions of the Waterford Crystal being presented to me after a beautifully taken birdie four. Then, thinking really big, I imagined getting the shot up *really* close and finishing with an eagle three. What a superb way to end it that would be.

So then I ended it. The sequence went like this. No backswing at all, just a dirty great heave. My right shoulder came round in an almighty loop, the club struck the turf two feet behind the ball, which then squirted off horribly to the right.

'Aaah, bollocks!' said I.

'Aaah!' said everybody else.

'Sshhh!' said the producer.

'What?' I said, genuinely innocent. 'What do you mean?'

Someone hissed: 'It's gone *live* into the hotel!'

'My God!' I said.

Peter Alliss spoke smoothly into his microphone. 'Yes,' he explained, 'it's an old golfing expression. It means "two down".'

That night I didn't dare show my face in the dining-room. I had become a hero with my fellow-golfers but a villain to all those little old ladies whose tea-time I had ruined, making them slurp their Earl Grey and drop their cream buns.

Later, though, one of them did smile coyly at me.

The commentators

Peter Alliss, bless him, at least managed to pour some timely oil on that little stretch of troubled water. In fact, I have nothing but respect for Peter and his abilities as a commentator – especially when it comes to saying nothing, or next to nothing, instead of blaring on like some of his colleagues, especially the Americans. In the States they have a horror of silence. To them, silence is like a hole appearing in a wall. If it isn't dealt with immediately, stuffed with verbal Polyfilla, they think they will get the sack. This is because the

91

Executive Vice-President of Sackings is even more frightened than they are of the public switching to another channel, and of the effect this will have on The Ratings. So, silence has no chance on American television.

Admiral Longhurst

Television commentators are powerful men, and their judgments can seem hard at times. But it is their job to be objective, to see it all and say what they think about it. Toes are bound to be trodden on. I remember all too well the day Henry Longhurst trod on mine.

Peter Alliss's great predecessor in the commentary box was doing the Pro-Celeb series from Gleneagles, and I was on the 14th on the King's Course – a short four which you can drive. Miller and Jacklin were the pros that day; Ephraim Zimbalist Junior and I were the ams. USA versus Britain.

I put my drive into a bunker beside the green, and Jacko said encouragingly:

'Just splash it out and up the bank. Then it will come off the bank and down again.'

Very sensible advice. Above me, as I went to play the shot, was the television gantry, and just at that moment I saw Henry Longhurst come out of his box for a breath of fresh air. He wandered along the gantry and stopped and leaned against it, surveying the scene below like an admiral on his flagship.

I went into the bunker and got the ball out, with what to me seemed quite a reasonable shot. In fact, I was quite pleased with it. I turned and called up to Longhurst:

'How about that, then, Henry? Pretty good, eh?'

He gave a snort of indignation. 'Hmphh,' he said. 'Bloody miracle.' And walked back into his box.

He was right, of course. That evening I saw the playback and my bunker shot was pure Charlie Chaplin: short backswing . . . whizz down . . . jerk . . . boomph . . . sand in the hair for anyone within a radius of twenty yards. Henry, who was never anyone's fool, had seen it all, and put the shot in its rightful place.

Miller, incidentally, had the audacity to play the nine holes that day in 29 shots. A privilege to watch.

The big matches

The major tournaments, and especially the Opens, now bring out the best, and sometimes the worst, in television. The British Open has become a super-event, like Wimbledon or Royal Ascot, where it's the thing to be seen. Attendance figures are up each year, and I almost wonder if it hasn't reached a point where numbers should be limited.

The writing has been on the wall for a long time; certainly since 1969. In fact, I have come to the conclusion that if all the people who have *said* they were present when Jacklin holed out at the 18th at Royal Lytham – if all those people really were there, they must have had twenty-seven million spectators round that green.

Going to an Open can still be a great experience for all the hustle and the crowds, and if you can get yourself a good vantage point – and are well supplied with life's little necessities – you can stay there all day and see the world's greatest players pass by. And that's a spectacle you will remember.

As ever, of course, you would see more on television. But, if you had the choice, wouldn't you rather be there? The televised version is beautifully filmed and, when people understand, as Peter Alliss does, that silence can be golden, it is beautifully presented. If only that was the whole story – or, as the midget said to Clive Clark: 'What's it like down there, Clive?'

It is all very well to say that we in Britain know how to do things properly, even if the Americans can't decide where to draw the line. The disease of Overtalk, though, is spreading. How would you like to be walking up the 18th, needing a four to win £50,000, and be asked by a TV man, who has just rushed onto the course, how you felt?

Sam Torrance could give you some guidelines. He had the tournament won. He was going along very nicely, reached the turn in thirty shots . . . then suddenly Manuel Pinero attacked. He shot a birdie, another birdie, an eagle. On those same holes Torrance took par, a bogie, a par. So in three holes Pinero had made up five shots; from nowhere, he was level. Torrance had every right to feel put out. But that was nothing. Up came a television interviewer – presumably acting on instructions from higher up – and asked him if he thought, maybe, the match was slipping away from him. To crown it, the interviewer then said he had been talking to Greg Norman and Greg had said Sam wasn't being positive enough, he wasn't going for the flag. Torrance said:

'I *am* going for the bloody flag!'

Well, what would you have said? I only wish it would happen to me. I would feel no remorse whatsoever in telling the interviewer to go forth and multiply – and not in the Biblical sense!

THE SAYINGS OF DENIS

Denis: 'I *knew* I was going to go in that bunker.'
A Friend: 'Well, why didn't you stop?'
Denis: 'I just *knew* I was going to go in there.'
He plays his shot; leaves the ball in the bunker.
Denis: 'I *knew* I was going to do that.'

THE TOURNAMENT

A week ago, I was in London. Then suddenly it was almost spring. Pack the shorts, the clubs, the wife and daughter. Down to Plymouth; ferry to Roscoff. Head for the Costa del Sol; stop near Marbella. The villa is still there. Good. Unpack the clubs, out on the course. There is work to do. Must keep ahead of the pack. Last year my team stormed through the field on the last day, scored 90 points and finished second. This year …

Lie back in the deckchair in the garden, soaking up the spring sunshine, listening to the 'heep heep' of the Spanish birds perched in the orange trees. In the background, a faint but strange gibbering noise. Ignore it; probably off a building site somewhere.

This year … Thoughts return to the tournament. We play two days on the Old Course at Sotogrande – perhaps my all-time favourite course – and a middle day at Las Brisas; plus two practice days to start the week. There will be fast greens and plenty of water. In fact, the words you hear most of all on the Costa in spring are 'Whoa!' and 'Hit a wall!' as putts streak across the slippery greens; also *'Agua!'* from the caddies, followed by

'Yes I know it's in the bloody *agua!*' from out-of-touch
British golfers who have never been in so many lakes before.

That strange gibbering noise I was hearing . . . it's getting
louder. What can it be? Now it's coming from overhead. Can't be a building
site. Shade the eyes and look up. Of course, it's Frank Carson, disguised as a
Boeing 707. His jets are screaming 'Gibbery-gibbery-doo' and

'Knackery-knackery-noo' . . . and he's coming in to land!

Yes, the lads are pouring in by the planeload. One hundred and twelve golfers, plus assorted wives, girlfriends and children. In three short days the gun will be going for the start of the 1983 Jimmy Tarbuck Spanish Classic.

An irresistible thought now springs to mind: how riled all those people up there would be if I could win my own trophy . . .

Sunday night

We are in a sort-of tent. David Steele, golf professional and one of the main tournament organizers, along with Ian Richardson of Benagolf, has just taken the microphone. His present task is to run through the basics of the tournament. Against a mild background uproar of glasses clinking, and a gaggle of comedians who can't stop saying hello to each other, he explains:

'It's a fifty-four hole, am-am competition. There are twenty-eight teams, each consisting of one celebrity and three amateurs. It is Stableford scoring, with the best two scores at each hole to count. The maximum handicap for gentlemen is eighteen, and for ladies it is thirty. All players receive seven-eighths of their handicap. The gentlemen will play off the white tees, the ladies off the red tees, and you will play the ball as it lies on all three days of the tournament.

'If you have any doubts about decisions on the golf course, don't hesitate to play two balls rather than come in for a ruling. You will find the local rules, relating to out-of-bounds, water hazards, and so on, on the back of your cards. The tournament is played under the rules of the Royal and Ancient. When you come in, I will be there, or Ian, to give a ruling on anything you weren't sure about.'

Next on our agenda is the draw. Now each team of three amateurs will find out which celebrity they are to play with through the week. And what a fine bunch of celebs they are. For the benefit of anyone in our audience who may not know quite what they are up against, I introduce the celebs one by one, adding a few random notes on their golfing prowess. (In the case of Kenny Lynch, the *News of the World* has just published enough about his other main hobby for my words to seem inadequate. All the same, for a man who has just voyaged round three thousand five hundred women, it is nice to see him so healthy!)

As for the rest, enough has been said, or will be said in this chapter, about Eric Sykes, Henry Cooper, Frank Carson, and some others. It was also my pleasure to welcome:

'From Liverpool Football Club, a man who played outstandingly for them for five hundred years – Ian Callaghan.

'Also from Liverpool, the sweet-spoken centre-forward who had the unique distinction of not being booked or sent off in a most almighty wonderful career – Ian St John.

'Behind the Saint, the big feller who made one of the finest captains Liverpool ever had. He led them up the steps at Wembley, down the steps of Yeats's Wine Lodge – they named it after him – Ronnie Yeats . . .

'A feller who has a wonderful restaurant down here on the coast. I tell you that because I eat there regularly myself. Also, five thousand flies can't be wrong – Tony Dalli . . .

'I am so pleased to see a new friend down here. He's shy about his golf, but he can play, and when I asked him to come down he was worried that the week would be too serious – and that's certainly not what it's going to be. Please welcome just about the greatest impressionist I've ever seen – Mike Yarwood . . .

'A man who came into comedy like a breath of fresh air. On the golf course, I wouldn't say he was slow, but if he goes out on Tuesday you won't see him back till Friday. Ladies and gentlemen – Jasper Carrott . . .'

And so it went on. We had a marvellous cast. We had last year's winning celeb, down from the cross to join us again – Robert Powell. We had Jerry Stevens, a fine player who won the Bob Hope. We had Mick McManus, whose Boston crabs were sometimes better than his golf shots, but a real gentleman for all that. We had Michael Medwin, Duggie Brown, Richard O'Sullivan, Bobby Charlton, Jimmy Hill, Roger de Courcey – with whom I had just been working in the series *Live From Her Majesty's* – Stan Stennett, and many others. I knew it would be an exhilarating week, and that evening after the draw many of the competitors broke up into smaller parties that went on into the wee hours.

Of the twenty-eight teams of amateurs who had come, fourteen had re-booked from the previous year, and the hotel where they were staying was filled with nice people who had a lot to catch up on. I sneaked off to bed, well content. I had already had a long and busy day and now also had met my team. Three Ulstermen – Ray Kelly, Callum Small and Des McCabe, with handicaps of 6, 7 and 18 respectively. On paper we looked one of the strongest teams.

That trophy, I thought, snuggling down in bed. It was far from impossible . . .

The practice rounds

Before the draw on that Sunday evening, everyone had had the opportunity of sampling the wonderful Old Course at Sotogrande. Teams had started going out from about ten o'clock in the morning, and an hour or so later I was teeing off with three friends from Coombe Hill – Ranj Anand, Chic Morgan and David Timperley.

They all take their golf seriously, though Ranj is in a competitive class of his own. At home he plays off a handicap of 26, but this has not deterred him from hiring Peter Coleman, who caddies for Seve Ballesteros, to come to Spain for the week and advise him on club selection.

At one hole Ranj asks: 'What did Severiano hit here?'

'Seven iron,' replies Peter.

'Seven iron,' mutters Ranj, a trifle intensely but that is his way. 'What do I need?'

'Four wood,' says Peter. 'Twice.'

It was a perfect day for golf, soft and cool, the temperature about sixty-two degrees with the palest grey cloud cover. Soon we had nearly all our twenty-eight groups out on the winding 6,810 yards of the Old Course, which offers a beautiful combination of palm-lined dunelands, hilly fairways going up through a cork-oak forest, then down again to the clubhouse over broad fairways bordered by man-made lakes which can come into play on five of the last nine holes. Not so far away in the distance, the great rock of Gibraltar stands up to the sky.

With so many enthusiastic but underpractised players out on the course – few British club players are exactly peaking in March – some mayhem was predictable. Sure enough, a report soon came through that Jasper Carrott had played too quickly at one and hit Roger de Courcey. (This was the only time in the week that no-one saw Roger's lips move.)

As for my own play, on the first nine holes you could not have called it better than patchy. A tendency to slice was being severely punished by the cork oak trees, which crouch in groups like slip fielders and use their gnarled branches to gather anything that goes off-line, especially down the right side.

Faith is restored at the 10th where, stepping out from the halfway drinks hut well primed with fizzy orange, I hit a blinding drive that fades beautifully over the trees and comes to rest well up the second part of the dog-leg fairway.

'That will give you gentlemen something to work on,' I

announce to the others, and step back to the drinks hut grinning like a Cheshire cat, then murder another bottle of orangeade, a bag of chips and a bar of chocolate while the others – less familiar with the route over the trees – take two shots to get up with me.

So we make our way gently round. At the 12th, the jumping trout are in great form, leaping high out of the *agua* and threatening to catch any low-flying golf balls in their mouths. Around this neck of the course, the water is a constant threat, and so are the runs of mole hills (Spanish rabbit scrapes?) which pop up constantly next to the lakes and make the business of dropping a ball even more of a lottery than usual.

Back in the clubhouse around three o'clock, and the waiters are already half on their knees keeping the tournament stoked up with beers, wines, salads, steaks and club sandwiches. One day out from the UK and pink cheeks are replacing city pallors. There is optimism in the air.

Next morning, after the draw, we are over at Las Brisas, in the hinterland near Marbella, on the Puerto Banus side. The sun is up and bright but there has been heavy overnight rain. On the many steep slopes around the course the fairways are soggy and muddy, and after a quick conference with Ian Richardson it is agreed that players should be allowed to pick up from a bad lie, wipe and replace their balls within six inches of the spot, but not nearer the hole.

This turned out to be a good ruling. For one thing, we didn't want to be over-serious in a week that was meant to be a holiday. For

101

another, it made life a good deal less frustrating for the better, steadier players who reckoned to land around the centres of most fairways which, in the present conditions, were liable to be the most churned-up areas and so give more bad lies than out on the fringes.

My playing partners for the second practice day are the Liverpool boys – Cally, the Saint, and Big Ron Yeats. That morning Yeatsey has turned out in a special white short-sleeved shirt with a badge in blue commemorating our tournament. I ask if it fits him, and am glad to hear it does because to get enough material to make it I happen to know they opened a new cottonfield in Alabama!

I also notice that he is driving with more than his usual unusual power. He hands over his driver, a kind of steel-shafted telegraph pole, and tells me he won it in a driving competition. At the 5th I have a go with it, and whirl round in circles like a hammer-thrower.

At the 6th we could have killed someone. The Saint hits a low drive. The ball screams down the hill, going a shade right, and then has a very nasty accident, thwacking with an almighty blow into the front of a golf cart which some genius has parked well out in the fairway.

'Fore!' roars the Saint, one second before the collision – or was it 'Whoa'? In any case, it is too late. We wait in hushed silence, half-expecting a stunned body to tumble out of the cart. When no-one does, the whole of our team falls apart on the tee.

The sun is now getting hot, and a small open-air spot in the back of my haircut is beginning to blister. I pull on my best tropical gear – a floppy white cotton cap (as worn on the front cover). The boys will like this, I think, and call up the fairway:

'Here you are, lads. Would any of you like to shelter under this?'

Big Ron is not slow to see an opening. 'Yes,' he shouts, 'I'll have one of those pizzas!'

Everyone laughs and we splash on round. Despite the heat of the sun, the course is taking a long time to dry out. From the ankles up, it's like playing in East Africa; on the ground its like a Northern Municipal in November. Something to look out for on Wednesday, when we come back here for real.

Day One

The rain in Spain has been up to its tricks again. As we drive down the coast road to Sotogrande, I peer through the grey murk and reflect on the wise words of Eric Sykes:

'If you're standing on the first tee at Sotogrande, and you can see Gibraltar, rain is on the way. If you can't see it, then it's pissing down.'

Over at the start, it's like the beginning of Ascot week – a parade of umbrellas. The Spanish caddies have not been caught out. They stand in a huddle, wrapped up like sardine fishermen in yellow oilskins and mud-coloured sou'westers, waiting for the action to begin.

Our rules committee take about two seconds to decide to play as we did yesterday, with picking up and placing. Soon we are ready to go.

First man to drive off is the celebrity of Team No 1 in the order, Johnny Pritchett. It is good, in these testing conditions, to have an undefeated European boxing champion to show the rest of us the way. Johnny, a 12-handicapper, knows what to do and hits a sound blow down the middle.

His team follow, then it is the turn of Team No 2, led by racing driver John Fitzpatrick.

The interval between the teams has been fixed at eight minutes. As the rest of Team 3 wander over to the tee from the practice putting ground, someone wonders where the fourth team member has got to. Soon the cry goes up:

'Find Carson!'

That quietest and most withdrawn of men has not only chosen this moment to go completely silent, he has disappeared! The alarm, fortunately, is short-lived. Soon he emerges, whistling, from somewhere in the clubhouse, strides to the tee and gathers his team around him for a last-minute tactical conference. Shrewdly, he keeps it short; in fact the entire team-talk consists of five words:

'We need a few birdies,' he tells them.

Moments later Frank is on the tee, waggling the face of his driver. It is still early enough in the day for whoever then farted to be excused for doing so. Frank barely glances back over his shoulder.

'How would you like a wind like that in your face all the way to Carrick?' says he. Whooomph! Away goes Frank.

The other most important Ulstermen on the course – my team – are out and about getting in some practice, but we are Team 22 and it will be more than two hours before we start our round. Meanwhile it is interesting to see how the amateurs and their celebs are getting on together. By and large the ams seem to be holding their own very well.

As with Carson, Jimmy Hill (Team 5) needs to be levered out of the clubhouse where he has found a telephone. With only seconds to go, he at last bounces down the grassy slope to the 1st tee.

Hill, rubbing his hands together like he used to do in the centre circle at Fulham: 'Right, team. Are we ready?'

104   Team, loudly and together: 'Are *we* ready?'

Nothing daunted, the footballing legend drives off. It could not be called a long drive, but it is straight and bumbles about 90 yards.

Hill turns to face his men. 'Team,' he says, 'that's just the steady start we need.'

Team, loudly and together: 'We said we wanted you to be steady. But not that bloody steady!'

Further down the playing order, there is some genial sparring between racing driver Trevor Taylor and Bernie Coral, one of his team members.

Bernie says, as they establish who should drive first: 'Trevor, you do it. You're the celebrity. Afterwards, I might ask for your autograph.'

Trevor replies: 'Afterwards, I might not give it to you.'

It looks as if nothing will stop the rain, and with the Stableford points system we are using – 1 point for 1 over par, 2 points for par, 3 for a birdie, 4 for an eagle – the general view is that any team scoring over 80 will be doing well.

When at last it is time for me and the Ulstermen to go, we get the start that every team has been praying for: we are straight, if not dynamically long, and walk down the 1st fairway with feelings of relief mixed with anticipation. Now we will see.

Meanwhile, at the turn, the refreshment hut and adjoining toilets are doing a brisk trade as the early starters complete the outward nine holes. First indications are that 80 will indeed be a good score. Johnny Pritchett's team are 10 points adrift with 30, John Fitzpatrick has 37, Frank

Carson 35. Later, helped by a burst of sunshine, the scoring rate is to pick up, with the high scorers mainly in the bottom half of the draw. For the time being, though, there looks to be no possible break in the weather. The sky is a uniform dark grey, the rain alternating between relentless drizzle and utter downpour.

The weather pattern seems to have seeped into the skins of the early competitors, who are heroically good-humoured even if the jokes are on the black side.

Frank Carson parks himself against a post on the verandah of the hut, looks round at the grim sky behind him and, while he and his team pitch into bottles of Fanta and bags of chips, launches a series of Man Near Deathbed jokes:

'A feller comes back from the doctor and says: "I'm feeling depressed. The doctor says I have to take a pill every day for the rest of me life." His wife says: "Well that's not so bad, is it?" "Yes it is," says the feller, "he's only given me four."'

Frank has been drawn with the team he deserves. One of them comes back immediately with: 'A feller has only twelve hours to live, so he says to his friend: "Let's go out tonight." The friend says: "No, I've got to go home." "Oh, come on," says the feller, "I need to go out." The friend says: "No. It's all very well for you. You haven't got to get up in the morning."'

The jokes perfectly match the mood of the weather. Frank goes on: 'A feller has only three minutes to live, so he says to the doctor: "Can't you do *something* for me?" The doctor says: "I could boil you an egg."'

The refreshment hut proves a great place for people to collect themselves and also to open out a little. When Mike Yarwood gets there, he has realized that he is in a golf tournament, but he has also now played nine holes with his new teammate Denis ('Sayings of Denis') Hopkins, and is beginning to accept that you can't win them all. Someone asks him which golf people he 'does'.

'Well,' he says, reflectively, also with a look out at the rain. 'I can do Henry Longhurst. But maybe I should do someone else.'

A spectator, right on cue: 'Who's Henry Longhurst?'

Yarwood, mournfully: 'He's dead. Like most of the people I do. And that includes the ones who are still living!'

If the rain is really getting into people's socks, it is having a different effect on the local wildlife. It has freshened them up, and each time a break appears in the clouds, they rip into their spring mating calls. Thanks to them we learn, at last, why Jasper Carrott is a challenger for the world's slowest player. He is about to drive when a bird sends out a wild shriek not three yards from where he stands meditating over the ball. His concentration shattered, Birmingham's answer to Buddha lays down his club and protests to the crowd:

'You see! They all do it. Whenever they see me. And not just birds. Ducks, hens, geese, dogs, frogs. "Here comes the Carrott," they say. "Roight. Let's give it to 'im. Gweerrk, gweerrk! Cluck cluck. Woof woof."'

Meanwhile, there's the Ulstermen and me. We are doing well, and the points are racking up nicely. At the turn we could be second. Behind us, and therefore an unknown quantity, is Tony Dalli, who will tell anyone he has scored nine eagles personally, but who could well be in the running at the finish. Also behind us is Ian Callaghan, much improved lately, whose team are currently the most fancied of all. And there's Bobby Charlton, who also has a team with fine potential.

At last, there is a break in the weather: the sun comes out. But it's a false promise and the rain is soon thrashing down again. However, when we reach the clump of tall pines by the 17th green, it is bright and clearing fast. We finish the round and walk up to the clubhouse. Outside, masking the scoreboard, is a reception committee fronted by Kenny Lynch. He gives me the poker-face and says:

'You look like you're in the high 60s.'

Let them wait, I think to myself. 'I can beat 80,' I say. 'I can beat 81. I can beat 82 . . . 83 I can beat.' (No reaction so far; what do they want, blood?) 'I can beat 84,' I go on. Is the tension mounting, or is it just me? '85 I can beat . . . I can tie with 86.'

We are third. After a day like that, I am well pleased. Like a lot of other people, we lost out on a couple of short holes but our scoring had been good. If we can do well tomorrow, hang in there, we must be in with a squeak. Yes, 86. I'll settle for that.

The completed scoreboard confirms that it's going to be a

tight contest. At the top of the list are:

1st	Ian St John	88 points
2nd	Richard O'Sullivan	87
3rd	Jimmy Tarbuck	86
4th	Tony Dalli	85
5th	Ron Yeats	84
6th	Jerry Stevens	83
7th	=Roger de Courcey	82
	Stan Stennett	
9th	Michael Medwin	81
10th	=Johnny Briggs	80
	Jasper Carrott	
	Ian Callaghan	

Twelve teams have cracked 80 on a very dirty March day. But who can do it again tomorrow?

Day Two

Las Brisas on Wednesday played much as it had for the practice round. Warm and slippery. It saw the downfall of several, and the emergence of a clear leader. Despite the odd conditions, some big scores were hit. One of the teams to experience both the plus and the minus side of this topsy-turvy day was Team 17, also known as the Stennett-Kravitz quartet.

Stan Stennett, that lovely sad-faced comedian, musician and actor, is playing off 18. With him are Messrs Kravitz, Newmarch and Jones with handicaps of 10, 11 and 13 respectively, which made them a powerful group.

Undoubted leader of this pack is the pugnacious Mr Kravitz, an old friend of mine and a fierce competitor. Dick is built like a Sherman tank and he speaks like a character out of Al Capone's Chicago, always chewing on a cigar or on the place where a cigar has just been. As Team 17 meet behind the 1st tee on the second morning, Kravitz briefly studies their card and says:

'Right. I tink we stardoff de same way we did yesterday.'

The team bow to Dick's wisdom and he goes into his warm-up routine, carving violent holes in the air with his driver. He is not the most stylish of players but he can hit the thing, and that is what will be needed today.

For the second day, the starting times are reversed, and Team 17 are one of the earlier ones to get away. At Las Brisas, the course goes out in a loop of nine and the 9th is played back to a green just in front of the clubhouse. When next they are sighted, Stennett-Kravitz are going great guns. Quite a crowd is gathered behind the railings outside the pro's shop, and it is a mystery that so many people managed to disagree about what happened next.

I was already out and suffering on the back nine – a saga I will briefly go into later – and so did not see it myself. But apparently someone gave Stan some bad advice on club selection and he took a 7-iron when a 9-iron was all he needed. The upshot was . . . an upshot. Stan's ball came flying over the green and, as the spectators all hid or flung themselves on the deck, vanished from sight. Everyone joined in the hunt for it, and there were plenty of opinions on offer from the spectators about where the ball had landed; but it could not be found. Stan's moustache and eyelids turned droopier and more forlorn by the minute. In the end the team accepted the far-fetched account of a 'witness' who said the ball had whizzed into the locker-room and then disappeared. For Stan it was a sad episode because, until he took the wrong club, he was strongly placed to score two points on the hole.

As it was, Team 17 battled round, kept their nerve and came in with a very respectable 83, which at that time put them in second place behind Richard O'Sullivan, whose team of miracle workers had scored 86, putting them eight points ahead.

Kravitz, despite his 83, was looking miffed as they walked up from the 18th green. The harder he glared at his scorecard the more disgruntled he seemed to become, until at last he growled to a teammate: 'I reckon dat's six points more we shoulda had.'

His weary partner protested: 'Yeah, Dick, but that's the ideal. That's playing outa yer boots.'

Kravitz reached the scoreboard. O'Sullivan's score seemed to make his eyebrows cross over for a while, but then he came out with a statement that everyone who has ever played in a golf tournament will know to be true. He said:

'Ya never know. They got more points, but they're in the lead. On the last day ya leaders can kinda freeze up, ya know? I'd rather be second and in contention.'

Just then, while the Stennett-Kravitz team were hanging about waiting for their morale to improve, an English lady spectator came up to Stan.

'You were diddled,' she announced firmly. 'That was a load of rubbish about your ball going into the locker-room. We were stood just above the green and we *know* it didn't go in there. It went round the corner in front of the verandah. Load of rubbish what they said. You ought to demand a replay.'

Stan's gentle drooping face dropped a couple of inches further. Dick Kravitz, on the edge of the group, was for once speechless, but he managed a wry grin. This kind lady may have wished to be an angel of salvation. The only trouble was, she was three hours too late.

As for Team 22, we had one of those days we should like to have gone home and forgotten about. Sandy Tarbuck, that was me. I saw more sand on the second day than Lawrence of Arabia. Good shots, as well as the other sort, were finding the bunkers, and if we hadn't had the steadying influence of Callum, our team score would have been considerably less than the 77 we came in with.

Anyone listening to our conversation as we went round could not have failed to notice that we were not all of the same mind. For example:

Callum: 'What's that you played there, Jimmy?'

Myself: 'Nine iron.'

Callum: 'I'll take four.'

However, Team 22 were not alone in their tribulations. Of the other leaders, Ian St John and Tony Dalli had very much the same kind of day as we did. And poor old Henry Cooper had a terrible round, finishing with 51 points. Looking down the list at the end of the day, I saw some other teams who would have echoed Frank Carson's verdict. After the first day at Sotogrande he said: 'We're so many points behind, we need a knockout to get a draw.'

After two days, here is how the scoreboard looked:

1st	Richard O'Sullivan	87	86	173
2nd	Ron Yeats	84	82	166
3rd	Stan Stennett	82	83	165
4th	Ian St John	88	76	164
5th	=Ian Callaghan	80	83	163
	Tony Dalli	85	78	
	Jimmy Tarbuck	86	77	
	Roger de Courcey	82	81	
9th	Johnny Briggs	80	82	162
10th	Jasper Carrott	80	80	160

Tomorrow would certainly be the pressure day for Richard O'Sullivan's team. But perhaps they had already done enough. A lead of seven points was a comfortable one to take into the final round. One other thing that struck me after the second day: all three of the Liverpool lads were in the leading bunch. Once a trained competitor, always a trained competitor.

Day Three

Down the coast road again to Sotogrande. Today the Spanish weather has pulled a new stroke. A sharp wind is driving down the 1st fairway and David Steele, on the start line, predicts:

'It will last all day and probably get stronger. It will knock eight shots off the scores, so 80 will be very good. I expect some teams will be feeling a little bit demoralized after the first nine.'

David knows the Costa del Sol golf courses intimately, so he's worth listening to. Another who knows the area well is Tony Dalli, and he too is convinced it will be a low-scoring day. In fact, on the 1st tee he is offering half a million pesetas to twenty thousand that no team will reach 80. There are no takers. If there had been, he would have lost – but only by one.

Personally, I don't mind the wind. At Sotogrande it can help as well as hinder, and I am hopeful that my lads and I will be up with the prizewinners. Even if the trophy is beyond our grasp, there are prizes to be won for the first six teams home. I firmly intend to be in there somewhere.

Two teams in contention for the wooden spoon are those led by Henry Cooper and Eric Sykes. By pure chance these old friends and rivals are drawn next to each other, and today Henry's team are playing in front. They are doing a great deal better than on their disastrous 51 round at Las Brisas, and at the turn have scored 39. This also means that they are in with a good chance of recouping what they lost the day before in side-bets with Eric's team.

'We had to take a lot of verbals yesterday,' one of Henry's team explains. 'They were semaphoring at us with ten thousand peseta notes.'

'What we'll do,' says Henry,' I'll wait here till they come in and tell them we've got 21 points so far. You all put on long faces so they think we're really falling apart. Then we'll 'ave 'em.'

Henry's team wander over to the 10th tee and Henry hangs about on the edge of the fairway, just beneath the verandah of the refreshments hut. A couple of minutes later Eric walks into the hut, sees

Henry on the fairway, goes over to the rail of the verandah, grins down at Henry through his Havana and says:

'Best golf I've ever played Henry! We're having a marvellous round.'

Henry looks suitably upset and gestures towards his team: 'I've told that crowd, if they can't do better than 21 points on the next 'arf I'm not going to play with them next year.'

'Twenty-one points?' splutters someone in Eric's team.

'Twenty-one points?' splutters someone else.

The news is infectious and they swallow it completely. As they start to count their winnings in advance, Henry goes off to the tee, smiling quietly to himself.

Meanwhile, what of Richard O'Sullivan's team up there in the lead? Bearing in mind that more tournaments are lost than won, would they dig in and consolidate, or might they start to crack? If they did, could anyone catch them?

They were the fifth team out that morning, so they wouldn't know how safe their lead really was for something like two and a half hours – the distance in time between them and Ron Yeats's team, now perhaps their main challengers.

Richard himself seemed actually to enjoy it all. He hit a few trees, and more than a few bunkers, and he didn't score all that many points – but it was no great secret that he hadn't scored that many points all week. His team, on the other hand, were playing like demons.

Their play at the 18th green summed it all up. Richard was in the sand to one side of the green. The others played steadily up to the green,

THE SAYINGS OF DENIS

On the morning of the third day, Denis holds a team talk. M Yarwood, E Parsons and Mrs P Tarbuck listen respectfully to his message.

Denis: 'Now, team. We're only 37 points behind the leaders. We must be in with a *great* chance.'

then Richard hit a flier which soared over everyone's heads and stopped halfway to Gibraltar. The others holed out, and the team finished with 78 points.

When they compared their score with those of the other teams around them, they found they had beaten Stennett-Kravitz by two points on the day, and my own team by the same margin. Seventy-eight was in fact a very respectable score in the windy conditions, which were just as severe in mid-afternoon as they had been at ten o'clock when play started.

The surprise package was Michael Medwin's team. From finishing in ninth place on the first day, they fell right away on the second day, then with no pressure on them whatsoever relaxed and had a final round of 83. This was not only five shots better than Richard O'Sullivan's team, it was enough to push them up to second place in the final order. If only they had been on the tee when Tony Dalli was throwing out his half-million peseta challenge. But they wouldn't have known, then, that this was to be their day. Such is the unpredictability of golf.

This is how the tournament ended for the top six prize-winning teams:

1st	Richard O'Sullivan J McMahon M Small B Reilly	87	86	78	251
2nd	Michael Medwin M Winterford K Barnard R Whiteman	81	78	83	242
3rd	Stan Stennett R Kravitz R Newmarch D Jones	82	83	76	241
4th	Johnny Briggs A Smith Mrs A Smith W Townrow	80	82	77	239
5th	Jimmy Tarbuck R Kelly C Small D McCabe	86	77	76	239
6th	Ron Yeats C Clapham S Clough P Allen	84	82	73	239

(Places 4th, 5th and 6th were decided on the final round scores.)

The morning after

I am sitting in the sunshine. It's eleven o'clock on the day after the tournament, which was followed by a gala dinner and prizes presented by the 200 per cent wonderful Miss Diana Dors, who just happened to be down here on holiday and came along.

Some of the lads did a few minutes' cabaret at the gala, and what for me was a great night went on in the ballroom until two o'clock, then – so I hear, for I went off to bed – continued in the hotel bar until after four.

Now some of the celebs have already flown out – Frank Carson to bring a little joy in London, Jimmy Hill and the Saint to prepare for the weekend's soccer on television. Most of the others are taking a rest day and will fly home on Saturday.

People have been saying nice things to me about their week, and some have already started talking about 'next year'; so Ian Richardson and I will have some planning to do in a few months' time. There is a lobby that wants to move into Portugal, perhaps to Quinta do Lago. We shall see.

As I look back over it all, I am struck by what an amazing week it has been for fluctuating scores. So much so that we even did a diagram of it. As this shows, teams that ended Day One in the first ten places then went in every possible direction. From being the leader, Ian St John's team went right off the board; Richard O'Sullivan's team were rock-steady; Michael Medwin came back from the dead, and Johnny Briggs also finished strongly.

That is the best way to do it: to swoop through the field on the last day. You need something to lift you – say a long putt goes in or someone chips straight into the hole – then you are fired up and off you go. The fact that you have started the day in a lowly position doesn't matter any more.

The way not to do it is called 'taking the gas'. A team start off so fast, they take the gas and get jumpy. On the evening of the first day they decide not to go out for a drink; instead they go to bed at half-past nine. But they can't sleep. They lie there thinking: 'Jesus Christ, we're leading! Eighty-nine points. If we do that again tomorrow . . .' And on and on till dawn. The next day, they're finished. I'm not saying that is exactly what happened here; but it is the sort of thing that can and does happen in golf tournaments everywhere.

Neil Coles once said: 'In golf you never know. You just keep going.' In other words, some days it will start to run for you, and from nowhere you can be away. Other days it won't run for you, no matter what you do. I know. As I mentioned earlier, Lawrence of Arabia, Tarbuck of Las Brisas . . . when you speak of sand, we have been there.

	TEAM	DAY 1	DAY 2	DAY 3
1st	IAN ST JOHN			
2nd	RICHARD O'SULLIVAN			
3rd	JIMMY TARBUCK			
4th	TONY DALLI			
5th	RON YEATS			
6th	JERRY STEVENS			
7th	=ROGER DE COURCEY			
	STAN STENNETT			
9th	MICHAEL MEDWIN			
10th	=JOHNNY BRIGGS			
	JASPER CARROTT			
	IAN CALLAGHAN			

THE SHRINE

No matter where you come from, or how good you are, one day you have to go to the shrine, the place where we are led to believe it all started. St Andrews. It is a fascinating course, like no other, and the more you play it the more you will love it.

Imagine the thrill on my début there – partnered with Gary Player. I was so fired up, the adrenalin was flowing so freely, that I hit my first tee shot fifteen yards past his. In his famous clipped tones Player said:

'That ball was smoking, Jimmy. Really smoking.'

It was a clear calm day, and we both hit our wedges to the green, over the Swilcan Burn. That infamous obstacle safely cleared, we walked up to the bridge to cross it and Player put his hand on my shoulder and stopped me. He said:

'Jimmy. They have all walked across this bridge.'

I thought about what he was saying. About the giants of the game who had all passed this way. Sarazen, Jones, Hogan, Snead, Palmer, Nicklaus, Jacklin, Ballesteros . . .

Now I was to follow in their steps. And so can you. That to me is the magic of golf.

Lightning Source UK Ltd.
Milton Keynes UK
UKOW022358041012

200041UK00004B/34/P